A BRAIDED HEART

WRITERS ON WRITING
Jay Parini, Series Editor

A good writer is first a good reader. Looking at craft from the inside, with an intimate knowledge of its range and possibilities, writers also make some of our most insightful critics. With this series we will bring together the work of some of our finest writers on the subject they know best, discussing their own work and that of others, as well as concentrating on craft and other aspects of the writer's world.

   Poet, novelist, biographer, and critic, Jay Parini is the author of numerous books, including *The Apprentice Lover* and *One Matchless Time: A Life of William Faulkner*. Currently he is D. E. Axinn Professor of English & Creative Writing at Middlebury College.

A Braided Heart

Essays on Writing and Form

BRENDA MILLER

University of Michigan Press
Ann Arbor

Copyright © 2021 by Brenda Miller

For questions or permissions, please contact um.press.perms@umich.edu

Published in the United States of America by the
University of Michigan Press
Manufactured in the United States of America
Printed on acid-free paper
First published July 2021

A CIP catalog record for this book is available from the British Library.

Library of Congress Cataloging-in-Publication data has been applied for.

ISBN 978-0-472-07492-1 (hardcover : alk. paper)
ISBN 978-0-472-05492-3 (paper : alk. paper)
ISBN 978-0-472-12910-2 (e-book)

Library of Congress Control Number: 2021939586

There's a thread you follow. It goes among things that change. But it doesn't change.

—William Stafford

Contents

Acknowledgments

I would like to thank all my teachers, and all my students, for continually showing me how writing can, and will, save us.

Thank you to my writing allies: Julie Marie Wade, Lee Gulyas, Holly Hughes, Nancy Canyon, Katie Humes, Courtney Putnam, Kristiana Kahakauwila, Kaity Teer, Dayna Patterson, Elizabeth Vignali, Jessica Lee, Kimberly Peters, Vicki Hsueh, Suzanne Paola, Bruce Beasley, and Sheila Bender, who provided a haven for putting this book together. We all need each other.

Thank you to the places that allow writing to happen, in particular the Helen Riaboff Whiteley Center on San Juan Island, where many of these pieces began.

Thank you to the Rainier Writing Workshop (the low-residency MFA program at Pacific Lutheran University), where many of these craft articles were conceived as lectures and classes, or in conversations over a noisy meal. Long live community!

I am grateful to the following publications, where these essays originally appeared, sometimes in slightly different form:

"A Braided Heart: Shaping the Lyric Essay," in *Creating Nonfiction* (Story Press, 2001)

"'Brenda Miller Has a Cold,' or: How the Lyric Essay Happens," in *Seneca Review*, Fall 2007

"Cables, Chains, and Lariats: Form as Process," in *Family Resemblance: An Anthology and Exploration of 8 Hybrid Literary Genres*, eds. Marcela Sulak and Jacqueline Kolosov (Rose Metal Press, 2015)

"A Case Against Courage in Creative Nonfiction," in *AWP Writer's Chronicle*, 2011

"A Case Against Courage in Creative Nonfiction" was reprinted in *Bending Genre: Essays on Creative Nonfiction*, eds. Nicole Walker and Margot Singer (Bloomsbury Press, 2013)

"The Case Against Metaphor: An Apologia," in *Fourth Genre: Explorations in Creative Nonfiction*, Fall 2004

"Collaboration in the Time of Covid-19" originally appeared as a blog post for *Brevity*, ed. Dinty W. Moore, April 7, 2020

"Durable Goods," in *Tiferet*, Fall 2008

"The Fine Art of Containment in Creative Nonfiction," in *AWP Writer's Chronicle*, 2019

"How the Lyric Essay Happens" was reprinted in *Fourth Genre: Contemporary Creative Nonfiction*, ed. Michael Steinberg (Michigan State University Press, 2009)

"In Memoriam" and "On the Power of Your Word" originally appeared as blog posts for *The Pen and the Bell: Mindful Writing in a Busy World*, by Brenda Miller and Holly Hughes

"On Friendship, Assignments, Intuition, and Trust," in *Field Guide to Writing Flash Nonfiction*, ed. Dinty W. Moore (Rose Metal Press, 2012)

"On Thermostats" originally appeared as a blog post on *Writing It Real*, ed. Sheila Bender

Part of "First Words" originally appeared in Brenda Miller and Suzanne Paola, *Tell It Slant: Creating, Refining, and Shaping Creative Nonfiction* (McGraw Hill Education, 2002, 2011, 2019)

"The Shape of Emptiness," in *Brevity,* ed. Dinty W. Moore, Fall 2017

"The Shared Space Between Reader and Writer: A Case Study," in *Brevity*, ed. Dinty W. Moore, Winter 2015

"Writing Inside the Web: Creative Nonfiction in the Age of Connection," in *The Far Edges of Creative Nonfiction*, eds. Sean Prentiss and Joe Wilkins (Michigan State University Press, 2014)

Preface to Writers on Writing

Jay Parini

Writers feel a certain compulsion to read as well as write, and often to respond in writing to what they read. This oddity of this compulsion caught the eye of Joan Didion, who said: "The impulse to write things down is a peculiarly compulsive one, inexplicable to those who do not share it, useful only accidentally, only secondarily, in the way that any compulsion tries to justify itself." The inexplicable nature of this activity, for those who don't share the compulsion to respond to life with language, may remain something of a mystery.

It should be noted that writers are, first and foremost, readers. My own writing life only goes well when my reading life is going well. That is, I write happily and with fidelity to my experience when I'm moving through texts by other writers—poems, memoirs, novels, travel books, whatever—that excite in me the wish to write, even to imitate what I read. From my own conversations with other writers over the decades, I've heard the same thing. Writers read to feed their own work. They read to find inspiration. They read to "steal."

Walter Benjamin's special angle on this deserves quotation: "Writers are really people who write books not because they are poor, but because they are dissatisfied with the books which they could buy but do not like." It's true that the books I've written myself have been books I've felt like reading and could not find on any library shelf. This could be said of anyone who writes a book, I suspect. Why else bother?

Writers pay special attention to texts, and their criticism often seems much the best writing available on any kind of writing. I think of Ben Jonson and Dr. Johnson, Coleridge, Matthew Arnold, Eliot and Pound, Virginia Woolf and Randall Jarrell—just to name a few of the great writers who were also great critics, perhaps the best in their respective ages. They read closely, as if reading instructions upon which their lives depended, aware that reading, like writing, is an act of attention.

This series is called Writers on Writing. The idea was to bring together essays by writers of some consequence that show off their work of paying attention to texts, which we interpret broadly. Even the world is a text, available to scrutiny. For the most part, the pieces in these pages will reveal the depth of a writer's concern for language and style, for history as context, for the concerns that inevitably arise in any writer's or reader's life. Perhaps the best work of criticism will always be celebratory, focused on the reader's delight in a particular passage. But the writing at hand will excite any number of passions, including sorrow and dismay; this is part of the reading life, and the writing at hand will always reflect a wide range of responses to texts and textures. Ideally, it will inform as well as entertain the reader.

SECTION ONE

First Words

My brother is swinging the bat and I'm bored in the stands, eight years old. My mother has given me a piece of paper and a pen that's running out of ink. I've written: "I HAVE TWO BROTHERS. ONE IS A LITTLE ONE. ONE IS A BIG ONE. WE ONLY HAVE TWO GIRLS IN OUR FAMILY. ONE IS ME. ONE IS MY MOTHER." The mothers sit all around me, their straight skirts pulled tight across their knees, each one of them smoking a cigarette. They look like the women in cigarette ads, their mouths lacquered with lipstick, and they leave smudged kisses on the filters. When they tap the ashes off with their index fingers, their hard manicures gleam.

My brother is swinging the bat and wiggling his hips on the other side of the mesh. "THE BIG BROTHER IS MEAN. THE LITTLE BROTHER IS SOMETIMES MEAN." Where is my father? I squint to see him near the dugout, his hands cupped around his mouth. My mother, she must be about thirty years old. My father, thirty-three. My brother swings the bat, and the ball sails, sails, sails out of sight. Everyone stands up, cheering, but I stay seated long enough to write: "THE BIG BROTHER JUST MADE A HOME RUN AND I THINK THATS ALL I'LL WRITE. GOODBYE." I stand up, too, as my brother prances around the bases, casual and grown up and intelligent, slapping the hands held out in high fives as he trots past third. The plate is wide open, the catcher already sulking unmasked against the backstop. My brother slows to a walk and casually taps his foot against home.

I find that scrap of paper every time I move houses, or when I decide, in some fit of self-improvement, to clean out my closets. It lives in one of those old-fashioned memorabilia notebooks—*School Daze* emblazoned on the cover, with large pouches inside designated for each grade. My mother stuffed these pouches with all the litter that comes with growing up: tissue-paper report cards, sky blue and filled with the letter *S* for satisfactory; school photos, my earnest, lopsided grin never changing no matter how much I grow; stiff cardboard programs from tap-dance recitals providing evidence of my part in "The Sidewalks of New York." This little scrap of paper—torn from a memo-size spiral notebook—has survived for over forty years, sandwiched into the second-grade pouch, the paper slick, the ink faded but legible.

Often, in my mind, I labeled this relic "The First Thing I Ever Wrote." It provided a convenient touchstone, a way to navigate my beginnings as a writer back to this small flag, waving me into home port. Here, I'm writing down my life: for whom I don't know. Why? I don't know. All I know is that it seems very important to get it right: the number of girls in the family, the number of boys, the indignity I suffer at the hands of my brothers. I need to record events as they happen, that home run now etched for eternity. I need to figure out all the parameters of this place I call home, to sketch them out in the open, where I can see them clearly. And I need to *tell* someone all this, and to let my invisible listener know when I'm through, when life itself calls me back to join it.

But now I have to wonder. Why would my mother have given me the pen and paper in the first place unless she already knew that writing would keep me happily occupied?

So I try to think back further, to see beyond this convenient myth I've created, and I find my younger self in the classroom at Andasol Avenue Elementary School, a name that this girl sounded out like an incantation, measuring her steps to the stressed beats—ANDasol, AVEnue, EleMENTary SCHOOL—as she marched down the sidewalk to class. There, this girl grips a pencil in her fist, writing her first words on wide-ruled paper that is rough and flecked with wood, smelling of the tree from which it originated.

Cursive. Just the word, itself, is magic; we love to say it in a whisper that implies something illicit, and I practice diligently, tracing all those curves, those connections. In the classroom the air is never so hushed as when all of us settle in for our handwriting lessons. Tongues stick out the corners of mouths, our brows furrow, we lean as close to the page as we dare, breathing hard, sometimes dropping our heads to the cool paper and drifting to sleep there, our arms curled around our few large words.

I'll eventually learn that Talmudic scholars used to write Hebrew characters in honey for their students; after the lesson the students licked the honey off the page, ingesting the letters. Our lessons are not as sweet, but at some point our alphabet, too, will suffuse our bodies. I know this without knowing it. One day we will simply transform into people who know how to read, people who know how to write.

I look up from my own paper where I've written my name and my dog's name, *Sheba*, and my brothers' names, *Gary* and *Scott*. The "G" was especially difficult and looks nothing like the "G" in my primer, but for now I don't care. For a few minutes, before the teacher catches me drifting and gently sets me back on course, I watch the heads of my compatriots as they write their letters, as they dig their pencils into the page and follow wherever they lead. I see the sandy brown hair of Jeff and Sam, the dark curls of Stacy, Jana's red tresses, and Valentina's silky blonde.

My first words are scrawled along the ruled paper, my letters drunkenly going astray. My teacher tacks my paper up on the wall anyway, our primitive calligraphy forming a border that runs around the perimeter of the room. *Cursive*, my teacher says, *is writing that is joined-up.* So every time now, when we enter the classroom—tired or hungry or bored—we look up and see ourselves joined, each hand merging to form *us*, our second-grade class.

But I know this isn't quite it either: the first thing I wrote. Before I knew how to physically trace the words onto a page, I memorized the sound of the chain-link fence as it rattled in the morning from hundreds of hands hanging onto it, and hands running sticks through it, and hands grabbing hold and shaking as we waited for the day to begin. I knew the sound of the tetherball as it smacked the pole that held it tethered, the sound of the rope slowly unwinding, then the whiz as it sped through a wide arc, only to be wound up tight again on the other side.

I inhaled the smell of chalk on the board, and the sound of my teacher's voice as she led us in the alphabet song. We chanted the rhyme like a vigorous spell until our voices went hoarse. I memorized the pattern of the dogs' barking on my way home from school: first the German shepherds, ferocious behind the wooden fence, then the terriers yapping it up farther down the block, and around the corner the ancient collie wheezing out his greeting and wagging his tail. I memorized the way the light shifted on Babbitt Street, how I floated through bars of darkness, then illumination. I knew in my body the approach of my cul-de-sac, tried not to blink as the Amestoy sign floated nearer and nearer, that harbinger of home.

I felt the difference in heat between the sidewalk and the asphalt of the driveway; recorded the smell of the garage, the oil on the floor, and the sharpened tools hanging in organized rows. I knew intimately the squeak of the vice grip bolted to the workbench, the way the handle twirled round and round. I knew the whooshing sigh of the screen door, the smell of the house at 3:10 in the afternoon, dust held in abeyance, vacuumed rugs with their furrowed rows, the brief absence of my mother, in another room, and the few seconds before her trilling *Hello! Who's there?* reached my ears. I was home, and yet not home, all of it familiar, and yet all of it new. *Who's there?* A question that follows me wherever I go.

Fan

I've written just a couple of fan letters in my life. I wrote my first when I was sixteen years old and trying to decide if I wanted to be a writer, and, if so, what kind of writer I wanted to become. Did I want to be a journalist? Or should I pursue more "literary" aspirations? I wrote to a local columnist in our paper, someone I read every day and admired for his wit and style. "I could be like him," I thought. My mother, with her trust that anyone will take the opportunity to be kind and of use, encouraged me, saying, "It couldn't hurt. If he doesn't want to be bothered, he just won't answer."

Being sixteen, I probably wrote an earnest, flowery letter, and I even quoted Kahlil Gibran on the necessity of finding one's true livelihood. I typed it on my mother's Remington, and she looked it over, smiling, made a few corrections in pencil, and I typed it again, folded it into its envelope, and sent it off to the *Los Angeles Times*.

I waited and waited for a reply, and to the man's credit, he did write back. My mother handed me the letter when I got home from school, the envelope thick, the *Times* logo dark with authority in the return address. I didn't tear into it right away, preferring, as I always do, to elongate moments of anticipation. But my mother was as curious as I was, so I finally slipped my thumb under the flap and unfolded his answer.

I can't remember exactly what he said to me, this girl who had written to him with such naïve hope that a single letter might elicit a response to clarify her world. He thanked me for writing, but then eviscerated my pretensions for going to writing school, saying that writing school trains people to write "drivel" like Kahlil Gibran's. Journalism, he said, was a noble profession, one that, should I decide to enter it, would hone me and keep me from descending to such levels of cliché. You had to be tough and clear-minded to see the world as it really was, not adorned with flowers out of season.

It was written with all his characteristic wit and style, and my face must have gone all blurred and trembly, the way it did whenever I felt ashamed, because my mother plucked the letter from me, scanned it, and said, "How could anyone write this to a child?" She threatened to write to his superiors at the paper, but I snapped, "I am *not* a child," grabbed the letter back, and squirreled it away to my room, where for some reason I read it again and again, the way you might worry a toothache with your tongue.

I wish I could find both letters now—my letter to him, his letter to me—because I think these two conflicting documents might actually have something to teach me: not about writing per se, or about the merits of journalism over literature, but about what my obsessions as a writer have always been. It might help me understand the open-handedness of that girl, her pleas for guidance really just a nascent version of the kinds of pleas for understanding she'd be practicing in her writing from then on. It might show me what happens when naiveté butts up against knowhow, and how the real answers lie somewhere in the gap in between.

Now, of course, I do see the absurdity and horror of quoting Kahlil Gibran to a hard-edged journalist, and I can understand his barely concealed exasperation with such naïve emotion at work; he was a newsman, after all, someone who expected the facts of the world to do his bidding with little or no ornamentation. And surprisingly, I think I did take his advice, harsh as it seemed at the time. I ended up an editor on the school newspaper (granted, I was the *features* editor, so my soft edges still showed) and majored in journalism in college, trying my best to see the world as a collection of facts that could be gathered and pruned. I reported on the visit to campus of one of the first female climbers of Everest. I reported on a Yurok elder's quest to have ancient ceremonial regalia returned to the tribe from the Smithsonian. I even did a little investigative journalism, reporting on a proposed logging road that would impinge on native lands, a story that made it to the front page of the *Arcata Journal.*

But my teachers didn't like me much. I kept getting A minuses instead of A's because I still had a little Kahlil Gibran in me. While I knew well enough how to belt out a lead paragraph, with clarity and panache, the typewriter's keys clacking away, I still wanted language to be beautiful, to show me something I didn't already know, to lead me to new truths that the facts alone could never reach.

So after I received my degree in journalism, I never wrote a newspaper story again. In fact, I hardly wrote anything for more than eight years. Language, and facts, had failed me somehow, and so I stopped speaking altogether. It wasn't a conscious decision; I simply drifted off into the inarticulate world, which seemed to do just fine without my words to shape it.

Ten years later, I wrote a fan letter to William Styron. I had found my way to writing again, and through grace and good fortune I also had a writing grant that allowed me to take time off for a year and do nothing but write. While this largesse may seem like a boon, it was also a terrifying prospect. I thought I had to do something "big" with this gift, such as write a novel, though I hadn't the foggiest clue how to write one.

So I sat in my little house in Seattle's Green Lake neighborhood, tapping away at my Mac Classic, and every minute the world outside called to me. We lived high up on a ridge, just a few blocks from the Seattle zoo, and on my daily morning walks I traveled through the African savannah, the Borneo jungle, and the South American desert. I came home and stared at my story—a convoluted morality play set in the near future— feeling completely lost. To be honest, I didn't even *like* writing fiction all that much, preferring instead the personal essay, but I didn't yet fully comprehend that writing in this form could be a viable, valid way to spend one's time. So slog away at my novel I did, and when I realized I needed help, I turned to William Styron.

I reread his novel *Sophie's Choice*. To me it was the perfect novel, the voice of the young narrator so sure and true, the horrible choice hovering at the center and shaping everything around it. When I finished reading it for the second time, I closed the covers and my present-day world seemed to have taken on both Styron's sadness and his joy at articulating that grief so well. I went out walking—through the zoo, then down through the neighborhood, past a house where the picket-fenced yard overflowed with dozens of whirligigs in every shape and color: ducks with wings spinning madly, rabbits with frantic pedaling legs, yellow petals of daisies a golden blur.

I had passed this house many times before, and had always stopped to admire the symphony of motion and color and sound, the way this menagerie seemed to give shape to the wind, happy to be subject to the wind's power. That day a strong breeze swept up the hill from Green Lake, and the neighbor's yard blurred in color and motion, all those ducks and hummingbirds and rabbits madly whirling, as if they might fly off their spindles at any moment and take flight. This motion, in light of Styron's novel, now seemed more frenzy than whimsy, as if these ever-cheerful creatures found themselves pursued by a malevolent force that could overtake them in an instant.

When I got home, I wrote to Mr. Styron, care of his publisher, certain that the letter would never reach him. I wrote to him about walking my neighborhood after rereading his book, admitting that my initial mercenary intention was merely to learn some technical moves about plot, character, and action, but then, overwhelmed by the book's power, I had to surrender again to the world he created, a world full of both evil and extraordinary love. I told him how I couldn't walk my neighborhood now without this awareness of an abiding darkness, how I came upon my neighbor's whirligigs and saw them as earnest expressions of goodness we try to make in the face of history's horrors.

I wrote it all, I'm sure, in quite solemn and flowery language, probably not much more sophisticated than the letter I had written years earlier to the journalist, though this time I was savvy enough not to quote Kahlil Gibran. But I did try to tell William Styron how his book reaffirmed for me that a writer's work is necessary and good; that I could now get on with the business of my own writing, no matter how bumbling it might be, no matter how much I might need to practice. His work showed me that it's essential to try.

I sent it off and thought no more about it. I continued writing my own bad novel, forcing myself to sit in my little room with the shades drawn, blocking out the world outside. Then one day there was a plain, white postcard in my mailbox with a man's spidery handwriting. Mr. Styron thanked me for writing him. He did not critique my writing style or make me feel ashamed of my extravagant emotion. He said that even at his advanced age, it was good to hear that he had reached a reader, that he had done what he intended when starting that novel so long ago. He wished me well in my own writing, and signed off.

I've kept that postcard for years, though I never know quite where it is. I'll find it when I'm packing up to move, or doing a deep cleaning on the file cabinet, and there it is, still emanating its simple and kind message, one writer to another.

Today I write in my attic loft, with only my dog and my cat for company. And I've just heard that William Styron has died. The news came casually, just another headline from NPR, half-heard as I poured boiling water over my filter of coffee: *Novelist William Styron dead yesterday at the age of eighty-one.* And then, just like that, I was sitting down at my kitchen table, coffee forgotten, my lower lip trembling.

With this news I realized that William Styron and I, we had a *relationship*, of sorts. Not an in-the-flesh kind of relationship, but one that might have been both more complicated and more endearing than that. We had the relationship that's forged between writer and reader, between writer and writer—the kind of bond we know so well as kids, that avid attachment to a writer who has shared with us the most intimate moments. Our relationship was all about words—his words, already so elegantly formed, and my own words still finding their way.

After reading *Sophie's Choice*, I had read everything of Styron's I could get my hands on. And though his novels are epic masterpieces, I found that one small book—his memoir of depression, *Darkness Visible*—moved me the most. His frank description of his mental illness, and the way he allowed me, the reader, to follow him through this darkness and into some semblance of light, made me hold this book tightly, to reread it again and again. His words had given me more than comfort. As someone who has since struggled with her own depression—and with the negotiation of how much to reveal to an anonymous audience—he showed me that it's okay to be honest, to be vulnerable, to be a human being on the page.

Today, I'm remembering my walk through the Seattle zoo, William Styron's words so vivid in my mind, the way he was like an apparition at my side, urging me to see below the surface of the world. I remember those whirligigs in my old neighbor's yard. I hope they somehow have survived all this time, wings spinning a wordless tribute up to the heavens.

Hand, Writing

Yesterday my computer broke down—my traveling computer, an ancient PowerBook 170. It's been making strange noises for a while now, the computer's equivalent of a portentous cough, but I blithely continued tapping away at the keys until the poor thing let out a death rattle and seized up. When I tried to restart, the hard drive spat and whirred, then feebly offered up a blinking question mark. *Sorry*, it seemed to say, *so sorry, what is it you want from me?*

Losing my computer feels a little like losing my mind—my writing mind at least. For over twenty years I've composed my work at the keyboard, and so I've come to see my writing, even in early stages, embodied in clean fonts—precise and authorial. The posture of my hands on the keys has become the stance of writing itself, a prerequisite for language to begin its long metamorphosis into meaning. Often I listen to Chopin as I write, the etudes in particular, and in my more fanciful moments I've likened my hands to those of a pianist: that same fluid movement across the keys, teasing out music from the letters at my command.

The enticements of the typewriter came early for me. I remember, as a young child, sitting at the kitchen counter with my mother's Remington in front of me, the "Learn Typing in 10 Easy Lessons" flipped open at my side and propped on its vertical stand. I felt for the small raised dot on the "f" and "j" keys that would align my fingers—a rudimentary Braille—

and typed "The quick brown fox jumped over the lazy dog's back" over and over, by touch alone, until the line seemed to appear on the paper of its own accord. The more I typed it, the more the sentence generated a hypnotic beat, becoming a mantra to unlock all the arcane secrets of communication. *The quick brown fox jumped over the lazy dog's back. The quick brown fox jumped over the lazy dog's back.* When I mastered this line I felt I now truly controlled the alphabet and could write anything my heart desired.

I wanted to be as good a typist as my mother; she could type 100 words a minute with no errors. She often sat at that typewriter in our kitchen, her hands flying over the keys. She'd had a lot of practice, in those years when a woman's prospects were largely determined by facility with keyboard and steno pad. Before my mother was my mother, she had worked as a secretary for *Seventeen* magazine in Manhattan; she often told me, wistfully, about dressing up to take the subway from Brooklyn to her job. I'm not sure what she had to type at our house, but watching her was like watching an athlete in her prime, every muscle moving in concert, with no wasted motion, no superfluous gesture. My mother at the typewriter became larger, sturdy, able to meet any challenge with aplomb. She rarely faltered, and when she did even her dexterity with the whiteout wand seemed world-class, a vision to behold. She leaned close to the carriage, brush held lightly between thumb and index finger; she swiped errors away so deftly they left no trace.

I loved everything about typing: the attainable goals of each lesson, each flip of the page in my lesson book a tangible marker of my progress. I loved the crank of the paper into the roller and the clack of the keys against the ribbon; sometimes I typed lines and lines of nonsense just to make this particularly joyful noise. When I ripped the sheet of paper from the typewriter I could run my fingers along the words and *feel* their existence on the page. They looked, in an oblique way, the way words looked in the books I consumed, with a crispness I could never get from my own hand.

When I went away to college I became a journalism major, drawn, I think, not only to the field itself, but to the rooms full of clattering typewriters. The machines endowed our work with a sense of urgency: not only did the professors judge us on how well we wrote, but on how fast we could churn the stories out, banging away at the keys. When we took tests for News Writing 101, the professor strode through the room with stopwatch in hand as we sweated to pound out the lead paragraphs on car accidents, burglaries, and murders. I always did well on these tests, pulling my paper from the roller long before the others, giving myself a few moments to revel in the sound of the typewriters around me, all of them chattering away in loud, discordant harmony.

My computer no longer even blinks a question mark at me; it has retreated into sullen silence and no amount of cajoling will rouse it. I'm in northern Wyoming—the "deep west," as someone called it at the dinner table the other night—and no one within 100 miles deals at all with Macintosh. I call Apple support on the pay phone in the barn, but as we speak I can hear the technician's tired sigh, the murmur of a physician who wants the family of the beloved to surrender, pull the plug, say their good-byes. But he kindly promises to send me a first-aid disk that might solve the problem. In the meantime, all I can do is wait.

So I capitulate to circumstance and get out my pen and paper. Not to say I've never written this way before; it's just that I've come to see writing by hand as a "minor" practice, useful for scribbling notes and lists, but not for the *real* laborious work of creation. I take a long time choosing just the right pen for this endeavor—a Pilot Precise V7—then take my notebook outside on the deck. It's a warm afternoon, a breeze rippling through the grasses in the fields that surround me. I write a little, I look up, I put the pen in my mouth, then lower it and write a few more words. I go on this way for about an hour, moments of writing balanced with time gazing at a nighthawk roosting in the cottonwood tree. Once I get going, the writing feels *leisurely*, there is no other way to put it: thought leads to thought in a way I rarely allow myself at the computer.

I think of Sei Shōnagon, a tenth-century woman-in-waiting, whose *Pillow Book* records a society bound by the handwritten word. In Japanese court life, men and women corresponded and entertained one another through the exchange of poems several times a day: a messenger delivered a poem to the house, and the occupant was expected to provide an instantaneous and witty reply. Shōnagon once received a letter from the Empress bound in bamboo, adorned with the branch of a flowering cherry; she penned her reply on the purple petal of a lotus flower. The outer trappings reflected the inner verse, a flowering branch forecasting the declaration of love concealed within.

Now, as I see my hand creating its own rhythm, I wish we kept up such niceties. I wish I had a fountain pen, so I could more fully experience the ink as it flows onto the page. One pen manufacturer compares writing with a fountain pen to "the way a race car driver feels and reads the road through the steering wheel." They often use gold for fountain pen nibs, soldering iridium or rhodium on the tip of the nib for durability. "In time," they say, "the nib wears just enough to the way the writer holds the pen relative to the paper to create a custom point unique to the individual owner." Fountain pen enthusiasts do not lend out their pens, for fear of ruining this perfect point. Just so, Sei Shōnagon used to complain of those rude oafs who asked to borrow her calligraphy brush, spoiling the perfect texture of the bristles she had labored to achieve.

I can see why. Already I'm enamored with writing with my Pilot Precise V7, a name reminiscent of a sports car, implying the same kind of handling, the same expertise. The pen and I now have an intimate relationship, my fingertips already a little callused. If I write long enough I will use up the black ink in the barrel, a sign that I've been laboring with materials that are *material*: finite and expendable.

The first-aid disk for my computer finally arrives by FedEx. When I put the disk into my computer, it tells me my hard drive is unreadable; I must initialize it in order to start from scratch, and this process will erase all the files stored there, files going back at least ten years, from my days in graduate school: the drafts of my failed first novel, notes for a ponderous memoir I've abandoned, correspondence with people whose names I now hardly recognize. I know I probably have these files backed up on floppy disks at home, but I can't be sure, and as for hard copies, well, they have probably gone the way of the trash bin in the many moves I've made since then.

I sit there a long time, the arrow quivering between "initialize" and "quit." I finally decide to do it. I click the "initialize" button. The computer whirls and stutters and wipes clean its own memory. The disk is now a happy blank, ready once again to be filled. For a moment I'm bereft. I lean back in my chair, my hand cupped over my heart. But in the next moment I feel an overwhelming relief, a *sovereignty*, as if I've freed myself from the weight of a barely remembered past, a past composed of megabytes, encoded symbols, hieroglyphics. I sleep well and easily for the first time in weeks after this annihilation. I know, with surprising equanimity, that *all* our work, no matter what medium we use, is evanescent: disks die, papers get lost, books disintegrate. All of it, every bit, hovers on the verge of decay.

The next day, my computer still does not work, though it's been purged of all that might have been holding it back. I don't have much time to write anyway; I've been asked to give a writing workshop at the local nursing home. Months earlier, I had gamely agreed, thinking I would teach spry women and men in their sixties, all eager to join in the class and write their memoirs. But when I get there I realize my students are very old, very ill, led into the room by their attendants, or pushed in by wheelchair. Some cannot speak at all or work their fingers nimbly enough to pick up a pen. They look frightened, bewildered, suspicious. We sit around a circular table, some of my students in nightgowns, others in clothes that have seen better days. Some have oxygen tanks on carts by their sides.

I want them to remember their first dwelling places, the earliest places they can remember living as children. They stare at me while I speak, as if I'm jabbering in a foreign language, but then I realize that most of them simply can't hear me.

"We'll *draw* it first," I yell, miming the action by scribbling in the air. "Draw the first house you ever lived in." I've brought crayons, and they bend to the task. Some draw very elaborate house plans, with blueprint exactness; others only a crosshatching of lines bunched into one corner.

"Okay," I shout. "Now pick one *small* detail that might have some important memories associated with it. Let's write about that memory."

One of the nurses passes around a vase full of pens, all with huge silk daisies attached to their tops. These flowers—red, yellow, blue—bob on wire stalks as the residents who are able pick them up and set them to paper. The room grows quiet, and then we are all writing with flowers, the petals nodding as if in a gentle wind. I look up from my own page and smile to see this field in bloom before me.

After several minutes they put down these lovely pens and tell us what they wrote about. One woman wrote about sneaking into the barn when she was five years old and starting up her father's Model T, then doing it again and again despite the punishments and threat. Her eyes light with glee as her attendant reads out her story. Stony tells his story in an endless loop that has no beginning, no end. Another woman, Gladys, tells me she had been given a certificate for penmanship when she was in grammar school, but *now* look, and I look and see nothing but a page of perfect cursive, neat and straight, betraying no evidence of her palsied hand. Another woman writes about spading the garden with her mother—not the produce in the garden itself, but the work of preparing the ground.

They begin to laugh as they listen to each other's stories, the air in the room finally lifting a little from its medicated haze. The flowered pens lie limp on the table, their work at this moment done. In a little while it will be time to gather them up, put them away in a vase where they will create a bouquet so extravagant it seems to give off perfume.

It's my last full day in Wyoming; tomorrow I'll pack up all my supplies— the useless computer, the idle printer, my Pilot Precise V7, my Cambridge flip-top Gold Fiber writing pad—and go home. To get myself in a writing mood, I skim the posthumous collection of William Stafford's poems, *The Way It Is*. The frontispiece shows a copy of Stafford's last poem, written the morning of his death. It's hand-written, of course: I've read that Stafford always rose at 4 a.m. and wrote lying down on his sofa in the den. This particular poem, written the morning of August 28, 1993, may not be a masterpiece, but written just hours before the poet's death it takes on the cachet of last words:

You can't tell when strange things with meaning
will happen. I'm [still] here writing it down
just the way it was. "You don't have to
prove anything," my mother said. "Just be ready
for what God sends." I listened and put my hand
out in the sun again. It was all easy.

Stafford crossed out one key line: "~~Time always attends our meetings, but never so impatient as then.~~" The cross-out makes me catch my breath; here, as nowhere else, we're allowed to see how the mind speaks, corrects itself, goes on speaking. It's really one of the better lines in the poem, and while I mourn its obliteration in the printed version, that cross-out makes it more precious, more dear. It links me to the poet with an intimacy the typeset version can never achieve. I become a happy voyeur, peering into this inked past to find the thought that skids through, wavers a moment, then vanishes.

The poet Anne Carson, reading the letters and diaries of Virginia Woolf shortly after the death of her own mother, turned to the crossed-out lines she found there for a type of solace:

> Crossouts are . . . like death: by a simple stroke—all is lost, yet still there. For death *although utterly unlike life* shares a skin with it. . . . Crossouts sustain me now. I search out and cherish them like old photographs of my mother in happier times. It may be a stage of grieving that will pass. It may be I'll never again think of sentences unshadowed in this way. It has changed me. Now I too am someone who knows marks.

Our handwriting *marks* us, locates us in time and place. Whenever we look at the handwritten manuscripts of the writers we cherish, we see more than words, especially when we come to them with our own love and grief so vivid on our skin. We cannot look at the scrawls, the margin notes, the doodles, and the bold crossouts without imagining the hand that made them, the living hand that leads to the arm, the arm crooked back toward the heart. When I look at my grandmother's handwriting— recipes for noodle puddings and stuffed cabbage, or the cryptic directions for knitting a sweater—these are the markings that carry her body entirely back to us. I can smell her perfume, Emeraude, in that ink, and the way it fades is exactly the way my grandmother fades into memory.

As a child, I had small, square book embossed with the word *Autographs* in curly script across the gold cover. Inside, the heavy-textured paper sat blank, waiting for who-knows-who to lay pen to paper and leave their trace. I understood the concept: an autograph is a souvenir, proof that you stood in the presence of someone famous, someone you want to remember. I know I must have collected a few famous names in my book; we lived in Los Angeles, after all, so it wouldn't be out of the question to see a minor celebrity or two walking down the street, eating in a restaurant, or getting out of a car. But mostly the pages became cluttered with autographs from my parents, my brothers, my friends. I held out the open book and intoned (with a slight British accent), *May I have your autograph?* And the autographer would consent, signing their name with a flourish: sometimes small, sometimes taking up an entire page.

I remember my mother's handwriting: so pretty and elegant, perfectly aligned. She used to write me letters, postcards, or chatty notes she included with packages, but I rarely see her handwriting now, everything replaced by emails and texts, everyone's words looking exactly the same. How are we supposed to hold them—the people we want to remember once they pass out of our presence? How do we collect them for future reference and harbor the traces of their bodies when these bodies are gone?

The Japanese calligraphers knew this; they said: "As every twig of a living tree is alive, so every tiny stroke of a piece of fine calligraphy has the energy of a living thing." When I go to a new-age bookstore I can try out this kind of calligraphy on a "disappearing ink board." I consider it a kind of Zen Etch-a-sketch; you stand at the counter and sweep a wet calligrapher's brush across the special paper. Your strokes register there, and you can admire them for a few minutes as they slowly fade from view, leaving the canvas virgin and blank. You can always start over. You can never preserve what was written on its face.

I find this a double-edged blessing.

Durable Goods

I.

Today I couldn't find any pens in the house. This happens quite frequently, no matter how often I buy the hopeful twelve-packs full of ballpoints, or a handful of my favorite Pilot Razor Points. After a few minutes of ransacking the usual pen haunts, I pulled open a drawer I rarely use and found it: a sawed-off white ballpoint, a pen an old boyfriend modified for me many years ago. These tiny pens were his specialty and caused girls not already enamored of his good looks to swoon a little and touch his wrist when he handed them out. It was a simple enough technique: with a Swiss Army knife, he cut the white barrels off cheap Bics down to a two-inch nub, replaced the black plug on the cut end, and voila: the perfect size pen to carry in a pocket or purse. It fits in the hand just right, the cap nuzzling the crescent of skin between thumb and forefinger.

K. must have given me the pen nine or ten years ago; he took such pleasure in making and giving these things, and I can imagine several different variations of the moment he handed this particular pen to me: while I sat at my desk in our house in Seattle, K. walking by on his way to the bathroom and placing it just on the edge of my desk without a word; or leaning over the kitchen counter with paring knife in hand, grinning as he dropped it in my palm; or in the car on our way to the health club, plucking it out of his pocket to hand it to me so I could write down some fleeting thought. That's the way we worked in those days, a lifetime ago: anticipating each other's needs a split second before we had to make them known.

I am not the kind of person who keeps track of things, even things I love. I've lost nearly every piece of jewelry ever given to me, including a beautiful gold *chai* necklace my parents gave to me on my thirteenth birthday. I lost the watch they engraved for me on my graduation from college. Within a week or so every pen I buy has somehow disappeared. And yet, this truncated instrument, this stump of a pen, has stuck around all these years, rising to the top of the heap, showing up just when I needed it most.

And, even more unlikely, it *still writes*. The ink reservoir is only two inches long, barely enough ink to sustain a few months' worth of checks, and yet here it is, like a testimonial, writing and writing, going and going, the ink still bold, the line still smooth, as if there will always be plenty.

II.

Durable goods are defined as products that are "not destroyed by consumer use," and newscasts often report on the sale of durable goods as a measure of the economy's health. K. always hated the way reporters felt compelled to give the definition of the term every time, usually adding that durable goods are meant to last at least three years. "Don't they think we know what the word *durable* means?" he grumbled, clicking off the radio. I never told him I wasn't sure of the meaning myself, that I'd always assumed most goods were durable, that things were, as the TV commercials often proclaimed, "built to last."

Beds, for instance. The first bed I owned stayed with me over ten years, and still sits in my attic loft as a spare: a queen-size futon, cotton with a wool core, that K. and I bought when we lived together in Seattle many years ago. K. built a frame for it in one day with wood trucked home from the lumber yard. He assembled it in the bedroom, screwing the sanded planks together with a cordless drill. He moved quickly, expertly, the muscles in his forearms tense, sweat filming on the back of his neck. He wore denim cutoffs and a thin white T-shirt, a Hanes Beefy-T that emphasized the biceps he carefully worked every day in the gym. I watched him from the doorway; he measured the raw planks, like Figaro measuring the space of his marriage bed, so intent on his work he remained unaware of my presence, oblivious, as men in labor often are.

As I watched him I was drawn most to the movement of his wrists. On our first date I was so nervous I could barely look him in the eye, so I kept my gaze focused on those hands and wrists as he ate his burger, drank his beer, told me stories of his life in New York as a writer and a carpenter. Those wrists were tapered and delicate; on this first date I imagined kissing them, placing my lips softly against his pulse. When we became lovers, he often stroked his wrist absently against my cheek, his hand tilted back—a gesture I found more erotic, more intimate, than the common, flat touch of a palm. Five years later, as I watched him build our bed, it seemed to me that all the force of this construction hinged there in the wrist—as he picked up the screw gun, held it tightly against the joint, put it down, swiveled on his knees for more nails, more wood, a piece of sandpaper, those quick hard swipes. Dust hung in the air around him, floated out the open window. I remember thinking this meant something: that somehow those hands built not only our bed, but a marriage, a solid place we could dwell in together without a thought.

The bed frame, it turned out, would be too big, too solid, too heavy— impossible to move from that room. Before K. left, he had to split it in two with his circular saw. I didn't watch. I don't remember what I was doing: packing books, washing dishes, lying with eyes closed in the hammock outside. But I heard the high whine of the saw as it bit into the frame, smelled the raw pine, pungent and new, as if the wood that had suffered beneath us all those years had never aged and all along kept some memory of its own beginnings.

III.

Recently, I ran into K. for the first time in years, at the front desk of a hotel while we both checked in for a conference. The hour was late, the hotel not quite up to snuff, and the lobby already held that simmering mix of anxiety and anticipation endemic to all such gatherings, people already keeping their gaze at chest level to read name tags, scanning the lobby for someone else. I hurried up to the front desk just as a man approached from the other side (I was already angry, changing my room, a list of grievances playing in my head), and I pushed my way in front of him. When I turned to give a hurried apology, I saw K.'s face grinning at me. "Well," he said, "I wondered how quickly I would run into you here."

I'm sure I babbled, and we stood a few awkward moments in the lobby, not sure whether to meet later for a drink, or just say our good-byes like any casual acquaintances. He is married now, with two children, and at that moment he was in a hurry to get to his room and wish his son goodnight. "I'll give you a call tomorrow," he said, "What's your room number?" and out of his pocket he pulled one of his mini-pens. At the sight of it, it all came back—all the best and worst of the years we had spent together, the meals we had cooked in our studio apartments in Missoula, the two of us huddled at separate desks in a house in Seattle, the bike rides to the health club, the fights in restaurants, the many partings and reconciliations, all the stuff of a coupled life. Seeing that little pen I had to catch my breath; I had to pretend I was busy with the straps of my luggage.

We never ended up having that drink, and when I saw him later it was only in passing, his face and body a blur, already gone. What stayed with me, though, lodged in whatever soft matter of my body holds such things, was the sight of that pen, lifted so casually from his pocket, and trailing behind it a wide swath of the past.

IV.

My little pen stays with me. I've been using it for weeks, and now it's a few days after the end of Hanukkah, a holiday that celebrates a jar of oil lasting eight days and eight nights, longer than anyone could dare hope. When we light the candles on the menorah, we're remembering the Maccabees, who drove the Greeks out of their temple but found it sorely defiled. To resanctify this holy place, the Maccabees need to burn holy oil, but they own only a single vial, enough to last for a day.

They've rebuilt the altar, they've prayed and prayed, the force of their breath scouring the place for worship. They're waiting for the holy oil to be pressed (only the first drop of oil from each olive may be used in the sacramental fuel), so they sit and pray in the unexpected light.

Do they think: *miracle?* Or do they simply expect it after all this time, such beneficence? To be a Maccabee is to be "as strong as hammers." They've fought men in greater numbers and survived. They've entered their stinking temple—redolent of sin, sex, gluttony—and restored it as best they can to a wan sanctity. I imagine them watching the sacred light not with awe or joy, but merely with a jaded satisfaction.

I'm not about to call my stub of a pen miraculous, but it does have a hint of the divine sparking around it: the way the ink refuses to deplete, the way it stays with me against all odds, against the pressure of the world to destroy it. And isn't that what we look for in any miracle? Don't we covet the lost body whole before us: durable and undiminished? Don't we long for the strength and stamina it takes to forge something holy?

Imagine: We stand perspiring in a lonely room, pressing single drops of oil from green olives, watching each drop accumulate in the glass. It's an exacting process, and our fingers ache, our eyes burn—it seems there will never be enough. The room smells of the olive groves of Gethsemane where Jesus, in a few years time, will preach a gospel of love, on the verge of his own demise.

His body, it turns out, will not endure, but something else abides, something else will lift into the air. In the meantime, we do what we need to do. We keep pressing and pressing, the flesh yielding so little and yet so much. And in that other chamber, just out of sight, the spent oil keeps burning. Any minute now, we'll run into that temple. We'll bear this filled jar in our bruised and glistening hands.

On Thermostats

Where I'm staying right now, at a retreat center in Virginia, I control the heat in the writing studios. The only thermostat for the building lives on my wall, and it's up to me to ensure that the heat is set at the "desired comfort level" for all ten people involved. It seems an odd and inefficient system—you can't ever turn down the heat, for instance, even at night, because you never know who is where and when, and so the heat must always whir into what are probably empty rooms.

You wouldn't think it would be such a big deal, this tiny responsibility, but I think about it all the time: I'm constantly pinging up from my chair to check the temperature, imagining the other writers at their desks, wreathed in scarves, rubbing their frostbitten hands, sniffling, catching their death. Or I imagine them sweltering, flinging open their windows and fanning themselves with sheaves of paper recovered from recycling bins. I hover over the small rectangular box, and I nudge the little lever to see if the heat is working, wait for the hum of ignition; I watch my own thermometer creep up and down.

Assuming responsibility for someone else's comfort or well-being: it's what I do all the time at home, and it's what I ostensibly came here to escape. Though I live alone, I have a cat to tend to, and friends whose moods vacillate, and colleagues who send a thousand officious emails adorned with exclamations points and icons of calendars, and students who are so tender I can sometimes barely breathe in their presence. Whenever I go on writing retreat, this sense of myself as someone responsible for others—someone whose gaze turns relentlessly *outward*—shucks away nearly the minute I step foot in my studio. I ease back to myself the way you might return to a beloved landscape, recognizing this landmark and that, eager to stroll down to those hidden places where you've always felt most at home. When I get together with my fellow colonists, I hear most often sentences that begin with the phrase "It occurred to me this morning . . ." or "It crossed my mind that. . . ." These prefatory clauses, while slight in an everyday context, reveal how the mind, given the right conditions, will become a soft receiving ground, so full of inviting crannies that thoughts, images, ideas can drift there and settle like pollen. And, like pollen, stick and fertilize.

But there's always something. A bubble of calm immediately attracts that which would make it burst. Calm, quiet, contemplative silence: it simply can't exist in a pristine state for long, even (perhaps especially so) at the places designed for such things. Emily Dickinson—that poet who went to great lengths not to be disturbed—once said, in a letter to Thomas Higginson: "The World is a spell so exquisite that everything conspires to break it."

I remember at the Millay Colony, in New York, the gardener made sure we came back to earth at 6:20 every morning by riding his lawn mower right under our windows, nosing the big red machine into the flower beds. Construction trucks rumbled past our studios, leaving a cloud of gravel and dust. At the Vermont Studio Center, the maintenance man decided to paint the trim on the outside of my windows during my two weeks in that studio, so I most often spent my time staring at his belt buckle as he moved up and down the front porch. At the Kalani Center, yoga classes blasted New Age funk rock music right outside my door, and the yoginis gyrated away, whooping and hollering their hard-won inner peace.

In all these cases I took personal affront, fussily precise about the conditions necessary to make writing possible. I took any opportunity to give up writing for the day once that illusion of insularity had been breached. Oh well, I would grumble, that's *it*, who can write in all this racket? I slammed my notebook shut (well, as much as you can *slam* two pieces of cardboard together; it makes a muted *whoosh* rather than an exclamative bark), or punched my computer off (though it, too, is decidedly unsatisfying when it comes to such things: just a delicate push of a button, rather than the thump and death rattle of an electric typewriter). I might stalk off to slouch in my chair (well, as much as you can *stalk* in a room the dimensions of a large walk-in closet, it was more of a *skulk*), to eat chocolate and read an Anne Tyler novel; if I'd had a TV available, and no shame about plunking down in front of it, I would probably have watched Judge Judy instead, marveling at her no-nonsense authority in the face of the world's foolishness. *She* would never consent to such a system. She would keep the thermostat wherever she damned well pleased, and if you're cold, well, *sue me.*

Here in Virginia, for the first week I was blissfully unaware of my role as Heat Queen, and my work seemed engaging even when it was uneven, and I allowed myself the kind of drifty afternoons where I read poetry, wrote a few lines, dreamed a few more but didn't write them down, just keeping the brain open to possibilities. I became both alert and languid at the same time. But this morning, Cora, the friendly housekeeper, and Bruce, the maintenance man, both bustled up to my room and said there was a problem with the heat—"people have been complaining," they said—and after a few minutes of fiddling with knobs and vents, they left, the heat blasting at a stifling 75 degrees. I know I don't dare touch that thermostat. Cora said she might come back with the key and lock it up so that no one can fiddle with it.

So, I sit here, gazing forlornly out my window, the heat blasting from the ceiling vent. I'm *this close* to stopping writing for the day, though it's only 10:30 a.m. But the landscape—with the Blue Ridge Mountains in the distance—seems not to have noticed the intrusion; the horizon rolls away from me in the same contemplative way it has all week, foggy and cool. The cup of tea steams at my right-hand side. My keyboard feels warm under the heels of my hands.

And my mind? I'm ready to feel that roiling disturbance, to feel put out, but maybe because I have a cold, or maybe because I figure it's not worth it, I just get back to work. I plug in my headphones, return to the soundtrack of birds and piano made by one of the composers in residence here. She has captured and amplified the rhythms in which these

Virginia birds live: the swoop of starlings, the red shiver of a cardinal in the morning, the wrens that hop every which way limb to limb.

Annie Dillard has likened the creative act to keeping a desk in midair by furiously pumping with our feet, maintaining the illusion that we're getting somewhere; any chink in the illusion and we'll come crashing to the ground. So those of us who have the privilege of a few unbroken hours might hang our little "please do not disturb" signs on the doors, or we scrawl in big letters, KEEP OUT; we set our faces carefully to give the right cues that we're *thinking*; or we plug our ears with noise-reducing headphones; or we sit in a quiet room with book in hand, fashioning a crystalline spell of language around our heads. But these, in the end, are all surface tricks, without the real bite necessary to keep our lives under control. Something will always be nudging at the door.

My friend Suzanne once told me about trying to write in her home office when her son was young; he would creep up to the door and whisper: "Mama, show you something!" and she kept turning him away, with kind and gentle exhortations to wait just a little while. She finally heard a slight swishing noise: he was sweeping a gull's feather under the doorjamb to grab her attention, and it worked; it was like being tapped on the shoulder by an angel. Another friend, a student, told me of the elaborate machinations necessary to get just one hour to herself, with the door shut to her study; she, too, heard a slight noise and turned to find, slipped under the door, a picture crayoned by her daughter: an image of a huge closed door, with a stick-figure girl in front of it, big tears falling from her cheeks. For myself, I have no children, but often I'll turn from my computer to a little scratching sound, and there I'll see the disembodied paw of my cat, upturned, sweeping back and forth, trying to snag me. For all of us, we could see these disturbances as both irritant and blessing: to be so missed that the world flattens itself out just to slip under the door to reach you.

And maybe, in the end, we just have to learn that there are no perfect conditions for writing. No perfect conditions for *anything*, in fact; maybe the best we can do is learn how to take each bit of the world as it comes, to have no real preferences, only what the Zen masters call a "radical acceptance" for things as they are. There are so many thermostats, after all, we try to keep calibrated in this world, and every single one of them eventually fails. We have that little thermostat in the brain attempting to keep the amount of information we can process at an even and steady level. And we have that thermostat in the heart that tells us exactly how much love we can readily receive, how much we can afford to expend. Our spirits try to stay on an even keel, no matter how many school shootings we read about in the morning's newspaper. We're careful to keep it all steady, no wild fluctuations if we can help it, but eventually it all flies apart, the thermostat busted. Or, at the very least, it feels as though someone in another room, a person oblivious to our plight, controls the temperature.

We can never be truly comfortable; that's what I'm learning as I steer my way into middle age: it's probably best, in fact, if everything is just on the edge of veering out of control. It's at the brink, after all, where our best work can be done. Cora's footsteps fade, the room becomes quiet, the only sound the heat blowing merrily through the downturned vents. I crack open the sliding door, and the cool autumn air slips in, my own little act of rebellion, of stasis. I breathe deeply. Then I sit down on the edge of my chair, and I begin again.

The Case Against Metaphor:

An Apologia

I'm on a walk in Point Reyes—a national seashore north of San Francisco—with a biologist. Where I see a generalized "nature," pretty enough, Rich sees a marsh that *teems* with activity: he points out green herons and yellow-legged sandpipers, Virginia rails and kingfishers, coots with white beaks, and a coyote with ears red as a fox. We see the coyote only because Rich noticed a deer, quite far away, who "looked kind of nervous." He followed the deer's gaze to see the coyote lurking among the trees. To me, all deer look nervous, but Rich has lived in Point Reyes for thirty years and his eyes, I imagine, are different than ordinary eyeballs—clearer perhaps, or wider—and his world seems more populated and friendlier than mine. We walk in that stance particular to naturalists, heads swiveling, our hands curved to fit the rim of the binoculars held against our chests.

He stops and points out a spider web glimmering on a bush. "It's the pumpkin spider," he says. It looks like an ordinary web to me: silky, luminescent, already a little tattered. I'm gazing around for fresh sights with my binoculars when Rich murmurs, as an aside, "The pumpkin spider eats her entire web every evening, then spins it new again in the morning." We walk on, but his words lodge—I can actually *feel* it

31

happening—in the region of my brain that makes metaphor. I know that eventually I'll return to my room and write this fact down, and it will steep in my head overnight. I'll get up and make my coffee and stand on the deck, wondering if the fog will lift, if today we'll see elk, if I'll ever finish the essay I've been mulling over all week. And when I sit down to write, the page will feel particularly blank, and I know I'll have to say something about the pumpkin spider and her web, because I'm a writer and that's what we do with interesting facts: we turn them into metaphor, we are metaphor-making machines. I know I will write something obliquely linking the spider's work to my own, something about how as a writer I, too, spend all day spinning webs, hoping to catch something substantial. I will wait all day on this gossamer thing, hungry. And at the end of the day I must be willing to eat this scaffold, make it disappear, and in the morning start all over again.

I already know this is the metaphor, waiting for me to grab it and run. It hovers in my peripheral vision, clouding everything, and I try to banish it for now; I want to just keep walking with Rich. I want to see what he tells me to see.

We see three wandering tattlers swooping in over the pond; they flutter and almost land, then flap up wildly and keep going. Rich tells me they're suffering from something called *zugenruhe*, a term coined by a German naturalist to describe migration anxiety. Though the birds have traveled all night and are surely weary, they can't bring themselves to land: their restlessness is too strong, the urge to keep moving too great. And already I can feel it, like a tickle in my throat, that strangled mandate: *Must. . . . Make . . . Metaphor*. But I don't want to, at least not yet; I don't want to make that inevitable connection between migratory fervor and my own vast restlessness, a disquiet we must *all* feel at one time or another: the anguished hover above a perfectly fine resting place. Already, in the instant it takes to walk a few feet further toward the shore, I've formed a notion of how we quiver and keep ourselves aloft, despite our exhaustion.

These kinds of metaphors—intuitive correlations between inner and outer worlds—have always exerted a powerful hold on me, and I'm not sure why. And I'm even less sure why I resist them now. There's nothing inherently *wrong* with metaphor: after all, there can be something edifying in the way analogy articulates what previously remained nebulous. When I see the wandering tattlers—and hear their story from a man who understands these wordless creatures—they elicit the sense of a truth always known but long forgotten. When I see the pumpkin spider at her endless and repeating task, she affirms for me that what I do every day is natural, almost preordained. These creatures, and the facts Rich feeds me about them, stay in mind because the links between us feel organic; my brain grows nooks and crannies precisely to receive these articulations. For me, it seems, there is no other way to speak, no other way to *think*.

One of my favorite poets, Jane Hirshfield, puts it this way: "My job as a human being as well as a writer is to feel as thoroughly as possible the experience that I am part of, and then press it a little further. To find out what happens if I ask, 'What else, what next, what more, what deeper, what hidden?' And to keep pressing into that endless realm, in many different ways." And perhaps that's it: by giving in to my metaphor reflex, I do pay greater attention to the world; I love it a little more. I see the pumpkin spider or the wandering tattlers, and they stick to me a little; I take a second look and then a third. When I'm in the zone—when the world appears to offer up symbols at every turn—I sometimes think I understand what monks must feel when they've solved their illogical koans: the grind of the brain ceasing, all things falling into place with a sigh. Even the dharma talks of the Zen masters use analogy or metaphor to clarify—little parables where every small object becomes a means to enlightenment: the overflowing teacup, the twirled wildflower, the ripe artichoke. All these things become portals for a new kind of wisdom to arise.

But today, for me, it all seems too *assembled*, and I want the world to just remain as it is, firmly itself. If, as Hirshfield suggests, my job is to pay attention, why can't I do it on the world's terms and not my own? Why do I need to push it further? Take my guide Rich, for example. His telepathy with the birds comes from his keen observations: he knows they are tired by observing them, by putting together this knowledge with what he knows of the season and the time of day. When he sees that they do not alight on the pond, he smiles at their predictability, the way they acquiesce to the patterns he's studied for years. Of course, I know his perception is as much a construct as mine, overlaid with the dialect of science, but his way seems more guileless; he has no need to *use* the birds the way I'm working them now, the way I reach out and grab hold of the tattlers for the lyric moment they may engender.

Today I want to see the world simply, plainly, without my writing hand limning every surface. Perhaps it's because I've been immersed in my meditation practice these last few mornings, ringing my little bell, and for a few moments at a time I hover close to that mindful ideal, each breath arriving coolly on the heels of the one before it, the world settling down from its constant swirl to sit quietly just as it is. The poet James Tate has written that poetry "speaks against an essential backdrop of silence. It is almost reluctant to speak at all, knowing that it can never fully name what is at the heart of its intention." Sometimes the open weave of the world presents itself, the empty spaces stretching wide, the silence a holy thing I would never want to break with my paltry utterance.

So for me, today, this reflex of meaning-making becomes a barrier rather than a path: a false illumination. Today I don't want to write the metaphor of the wandering tattlers, or all the others that now seem to throw themselves at me with reckless abandon. On the radio when I get home, I hear about freshwater eels, all of whom breed in the Sargasso Sea off Bermuda, then migrate to freshwater rivers all over North America. Ten or fifteen or twenty years later, they make their way thousands of miles back to the Sargasso, divesting themselves of their digestive system to make room for their growing sexual organs. Or I keep watching the Forster's tern this afternoon, how she keeps circling the pond at Tomales Bay, solitary hunter, diving again and again at the skin of water but coming up empty-taloned every time. Or the way the paths on the cliff keep diverging in the dried grass, all of them well-trod, most of them leading nowhere.

All these things register. The eels with their empty bellies. The estuary out my window and how it shows so clearly the transitions from sea to bay to river—each margin becomes a new ecotone altogether, and Rich says, "it all has to do with salt." And before the words are barely out of his mouth I'm thinking, of course, tears and sweat and our bodies, too, must have these tidal zones, different measures of salinity and all manner of life they're able to support....

And I say: *Enough!* Let salt be salt. Let the eels be eels and the web a web, let the tattlers fly all night and day; let the bay and estuary flow where they will, around and beyond the headland where the paths lead back the way they came. A world without metaphor, I imagine, would hold us in rapture, and, like rapture, would be beautiful, terrifying, and impossible to sustain. I know this afternoon I'll walk down to that cliff; I'll find the bend to the path where I can turn to look back on this house. I'll raise my binoculars, and see, in sharp focus, this balcony and this climbing rose, this rocking chair, and barely—like a ghost, like a shade— the faint contour of a person bent over her notebook, writing it all down.

SECTION TWO

A Braided Heart:

Shaping the Lyric Essay

On the first day of my class "Writing the Lyric Essay" I bring in a loaf of challah, the braided bread traditionally eaten for the Jewish Sabbath dinner. I take it out of my bag and set it in on a white cloth at the center of the table. Before I say anything at all about it, I watch my students' reactions: some eye it warily, some avoid looking at it altogether, and some seem delighted, hunger evident in their eyes.

I pass out the syllabus and watch the stapled packets make a circuit around the room, the challah still sitting placidly in the center of the table, innocuous yet full of mysterious power. I don't talk about the bread, but I begin some forays into the "lyric essay" in general. What is it? That is the main question we all have; I might even write it on the board. *What is the lyric essay?* Not only *what is it?* But *how do I make it?* What's the definition? What's the answer?

And I might tell them: *I don't know.* I might tell them, though they won't want to hear it, that we've entered a realm of unknowing, a place where definitions are constantly in flux, a place where answers are not as important as the questions to which they give rise.

THE CHALLAH

I loved challah when I was a child. It had to be bought from a special kosher bakery, the "Delicious Bakery" in the Hughes Shopping Center, and we had to get there at just the right time on Friday afternoons: before the loaves were sold out, and after they had just come from the oven, still warm, the egg wash and the sesame seed gleaming like gold. They seemed, in fact, the golden loaves of some fairy tale, minted from a factory deep inside a hidden cave, emerging on a conveyer belt and counted out for all the Jews of Northridge. There were a good many conservative congregations in the San Fernando Valley, the "California Jews" whom the East Coast Jews frowned upon, or dismissed. There's a joke: California Jews are not really Jews, they're Jew-*ish*.

And I suppose my family fit that description. We went to synagogue when necessary, and my brothers and I went to Hebrew school; I thought the men looked both distinguished and ridiculous with their yarmulkes on, the contrast between the elegant black silk and the womanish bobby pins used to hold them in place. My brothers took them off as soon as they could, but sometimes my father absentmindedly left his yarmulke on throughout the rest of that sanctified day, preoccupied with a piece of wood in his vise on the bench in the garage, or sitting with his feet up on the recliner, watching a Lakers game, waiting for dinner to be served.

Though we were secular Jews, we were still Jewish enough to appreciate the quality of the Sabbath bread, that beautiful, glowing challah. I recently asked a rabbi on the internet why the challah is braided, what is symbolic about it, and his email reply said (in a voice so much like those of the rabbis of my youth! Slightly contemptuous, a little annoyed . . .) that the Sabbath bread must only look *different* than everyday bread, that it need not be braided; it could be circular or oblong or in a rhomboid shape, for that matter. The braid had become custom for eastern European Jews; some bakers used three strands, some four; this rabbi, he said with a hint of pride, used six!

As a child, I knew only that the braided bread simply tasted *better* than ordinary bread, the way texture will often affect flavor, and the way presentation and form can sometimes, themselves, offer sustenance. I loved watching my mother cut through that jeweled crust, the heft of the buttered slice in my hands, the convoluted, lacquered outer surface giving way to the dense bread beneath. The inside was moist and delicious, tasted like an entire meal in itself. I often closed my eyes when I bit into it. Here was a bread that spoke of what it meant to have a sacred day: to bring the divine into one's small and common body.

BRAIDING THE CHALLAH

Divide the dough into four equal portions; roll each between your hands to form a strand about twenty inches long. Place the four strips lengthwise on a greased baking sheet, pinch the tops together, and braid as follows: pick up the strand on the right, bring it over the next one, under the third, and over the fourth. Repeat, always starting with the strand on the right, until the braid is complete. Pinch the ends together. Cover and let rise in a warm place until almost doubled. Using a soft brush or your fingers, spread an egg yolk mixture evenly over the braids; sprinkle with seed. Bake in a 350° oven for thirty to thirty-five minutes or until the loaf is golden brown and sounds hollow when tapped.

THE LYRIC ESSAY

"Lyric. Essay. How do you think the two fit together?" My students mull over the question, avoiding my eyes, their gaze landing on the glowing challah at the center of the table. "What would be the recipe for a lyric essay?" I ask. "What are the ingredients?"

"Imagery?" one student tentatively offers. I nod my head and lean forward in my chair. "Poetic language?" another asks. I get up and start writing on the board, as my students begin to call out words and phrases; *fragments, personal experience, metaphor, sentences, gaps, structure, white space, thesis, sensuality, voice, meditation, repetition, rhythm* . . . When we're done I have a blackboard full of possibilities, really a panoply of all the ways of writing itself. It's a little daunting. I sit down and ask them again: so what makes the lyric essay a lyric? What makes it an essay? Why not just write a poem, instead, if you want to be lyrical? Why not just write an essay, if you want to be prosaic?

Silence falls, so I tell my students that the lyric essay is quite an ancient form; it's nothing new. Writers such as Seneca, Bacon, Sei Shōnagon in the tenth century, Montaigne, and hundreds of others all could be said to write essays whose forms were inherently lyric. That is, they did not necessarily follow a linear, narrative line. Many excellent writers and thinkers have tried to pin down the lyric essay, defining it as a collage, a montage, a mosaic. It's been called disjunctive, paratactic, segmented, sectioned. All of these are correct. All of these recognize in the lyric essay a tendency toward fragmentation that invites the reader into those gaps, that emphasizes what is unknown rather than the already-articulated known. By infusing prose with tools normally relegated to the poetic sensibility, the lyric essayist creates anew, each time, a form that is interactive, alive, full of new spaces in which meaning can germinate. *The Seneca Review*, in its thirtieth anniversary issue devoted to lyric essays, characterized them as having "this built-in mechanism for provoking meditation. They require us to complete their meaning."

So, I underline *fragmentation* on the board. I underline the word *gaps*. I write the words *explode the narrative line!!* over the whole thing. My students nod; they write this down.

Then I go over and, with chalky hands, pick up the bread.

THE BRAIDED ESSAY

Writing has always—and always will, I'm sure—scared the hell out of me. I'll do just about anything to get out of it, and have been known to spend whole afternoons circling my desk like a dog, wary, unwilling to commit to writing a single word. What is so frightening about it? I still don't know. Perhaps it's the horrible knowledge that no matter how well you write, the resultant product will never correlate exactly to the truth, will never arrive with quite the melodious voice you hear in the acoustic cavity of your mind.

When I first started writing personal essays, I didn't know that's what

I was doing. I had written poetry for many years, but at some point felt restricted by the poetic line. So I started wandering past the line break and ended up writing autobiographical prose that had a lilting, hesitant quality to it, as if it still didn't trust itself in this unfenced yard.

But what I found was that this yard had just as many fences, just as many restrictions. I was struggling to write an essay that seemed very important to me, an essay about being a massage therapist for several years at a small hot-springs resort in northern California. This work had defined me and created a purpose based on serving others. By the time I was writing the essay, in 1989, this purpose had dissolved: I no longer practiced massage, and had yet to find another guiding principle to replace it. The urge to write was the urge to explain the sense of loss I felt, to bring coherence to an identity that now seemed fragmented, in flux, chaotic.

While I wrote, I kept looking at a photograph of myself from that time: I'm naked, in the hot tub of Orr Springs. The photographer (my boyfriend) chose to frame this scene through a windowpane misty with steam; we get a fragment of a jasmine bush, the blur of the water, my hands lifted to shield my face. The diffuse light centers on my abdomen (the site, it turns out, where much of my autobiographical material resides). I looked at this picture often, much the way I might gaze in a mirror: looking for a way into this body, a way for this image of the body to give up its secrets and make itself manifest in language. But as I tried to order this material of memory and image into a logical, linear narrative, the essay became flat, intractable, stubbornly refusing to yield any measure of truth.

By chance, I happened to be studying the personal essay form for an independent study class at the University of Montana. One of my classmates brought in an essay by the poet Albert Goldbarth. It was called "After Yitzl," and I had never read anything like it. Written in numbered sections that at first seem to have little do with one another, the essay worked through a steady accretion of imagery and key repetitions; it spoke in a voice that grew loud, then whispered, that cut itself off, then rambled. I found myself tripping over the gaps, then laughing delightedly as I found myself sprawled on the ground. Something cracked open inside me. I saw how cavalierly Goldbarth had exploded his prose in order to put it together again in a new pattern that was inordinately pleasurable.

So I turned to my own essay and tried the same thing. I deserted a narrative line in favor of images that intuitively rose up in the work. I allowed for silence, the caesuras between words, and the essay began to take on voices that hardly belonged to me. This fragmentation allowed for those moments of "not knowing," which to me became the most honest moments in the essay. I abandoned my authority, and with that surrender came great freedom: I no longer had to know the answers. I didn't have to come to a static conclusion. Instead, the essay began to make an intuitive kind of sense.

When I arrived at the final draft, I had fragmented three different narratives—my work as a massage therapist, the story of a life-threatening miscarriage, and the birth of my godson. All of this material was highly emotional to me; the fragmentation, however, allowed me—almost forced me—not to approach this material head-on, but to search for a more circuitous way into the essay. I had to expand my peripheral vision, to focus on images that at first seemed oblique to the stories. Sometimes our peripheral vision catches the most important details, those you might not have expected to carry significance. You give yourself over to chance sightings, arresting the image just as it's on the verge of skittering away. In the resultant essay, "A Thousand Buddhas," it was the image of my hands, those hands fluttering up in the photograph, that became a contextualizing force, yoking together the juxtaposed meditations on birth and death that surrounded it.

TAKING RISKS

For many bakers, kneading the soft dough is a lovely sensation, a sort of relaxing therapy. For others, the glorious moment comes with the first buttered bite of the fresh warm loaf. For everyone, the yeasty aroma wafting from the oven as the bread bakes crowns the day with a sense of delicious achievement. . . .

Yeast bread baking has the reputation of being chancy and difficult. . . . It's true that you do need to be careful at first. You have to protect the baby dough to get it started. But after that the bread almost makes itself.

MAKING CHALLAH

There was a time in my life when I made all my own bread. I loved every part of it: reading the recipes, gathering the ingredients, kneading the dough, allowing it to rise. And all the praise I reaped from the task didn't hurt either. I remember, when I was in college, laying out perfectly browned loaves of whole-wheat French bread on the kitchen counter in a house I shared with four men in Blue Lake; such love in their eyes, such devotion! I remember baking bread every day for children in a summer camp: big, oversized loaves of white bread that we cut and spread with churned butter. And the challah, of course: sometimes I got ambitious and tried the kind of loaves you saw in synagogue: a four-strand base, with a smaller, three-strand braid on top, so that the whole thing became a monstrous labyrinth. Mine always emerged a little lopsided, but that only added to its charm.

All good bread makers develop a finely honed sense of intuition that comes into play at every step of the process: knowing exactly the temperature of the water in which to proof your yeast, testing it not with a thermometer but against the most sensitive skin on the underside of your wrist, with the same thoughtful stance as a mother testing a baby's formula. You add the warm milk, the butter, the salt, a bit of sugar. After a while you stop measuring the flour as you stir, knowing the correct texture through the way it resists your arm. You take the sticky dough in your hands and knead, folding the dough toward you, then pushing away with the heel of your hand, turning and repeating, working and working with your entire body—your legs, your abdomen, your strong heart. You work the dough until it takes on the texture of satin. You poke it with your index finger and it sighs against your touch.

You cover it and let it rise. You keep it in your mind as it combusts in the warm dark. You return to it, this living thing you've created with your hands. You shape it to please the eye and the mouth. You pull it apart and roll the dough into yeasty ropes and begin to braid it back into a different form. You hope it will come out all right, that the strands aren't too thick or too thin, that they aren't too long or too short, that they won't fall apart in the middle, or break. Sometimes you have to unravel what you've done, start again. You keep braiding with your heart in your throat, hoping for the best. You have the egg wash at the ready, to add the finishing touches, the small bowl of poppy seeds. In your mind you have a vision of the perfect challah, gleaming on its special platter.

You do what you can. At some point the bread *almost makes itself*.

FRENCH BRAIDS

When I first met my boyfriend's daughters, Hannah and Sarah, the way into their hearts was to plait their hair in French braids. They had faith that all women over a certain age were able to braid hair, and so when they came to me with combs and ribbons in hand, I didn't have the heart to disillusion them. It was like a test of my merit as an adult female companion, and their eyes were so eager, so trusting: how could I refuse?

But braiding hair is not as easy as braiding bread. Especially French braids, which require a certain dexterity of the fingers, an intuitive feel for the slippery hair of young girls. The hair slides from the fingers, breaks off, becomes unruly. I had to start over, again and again, and when I was finished they looked terrible, not really like braids at all but like some old sailor's rope, knotted and twisted and frayed.

But the girls were satisfied enough. They ran to the mirror and tilted their heads; luckily they couldn't see all the way around to the back. They patted their hair as if it were a nice, strange new animal and thanked me for my trouble. I knew why they wanted it so badly: braided hair has an allure so much more exciting than "normal" hair, it has texture and substance and mystery. Where does one strand originate and the next one begin? The eye travels, dizzy with delight, over the highlights and the hair seems to shimmer more fully, takes on a coy illumination that beckons the hand to touch, to feel, to love.

THE BRAIDED ESSAY

After that first essay, "A Thousand Buddhas," I began to adopt the structure of fragmented, numbered sections for much of my prose. And I began to see more clearly that this form wasn't just about fragmentation and juxtaposition; it wasn't really mosaic I was after. There was more of a sense of weaving about it, of interruption and continuation, like the braiding of bread, or of hair. I had to keep my eye on the single strands that came in and out of focus, filaments that glinted differently depending on where they had been. At the same time, I had to keep my eye focused on the single image that held them all together.

As I began to adopt the braided essay more and more in my work, a strange, wonderful, and mysterious thing began to happen. While I was still writing "personal" essays, essays that mainly relied for their material on the experiences of my life, I found that they started to expand more outward, taking on myriad facts and stories of the outer world as well as the inner. New strands began to develop, but they still intersected with the memories most important to me. I liked this. It was as if I were creating the more complex, double-braided bread of the synagogue.

For instance, while at my first writing colony on an island in the Puget Sound, I happened to pick up an encyclopedia of Jewish religion from the library in the farmhouse. "Happened to" is the key phrase here; of my own essays, the ones I like the best arise out of happenstance, out of the material finding its way into my hands rather than vice versa. We must train ourselves into this state of "meditative expectancy," as Carolyn Forché calls the writer's stance; the world, after all, flies by us at millions of miles an hour, spewing out any number of offerings—it is the writer at her desk, the artist out perambulating, who will recognize a gift when she sees one. As I turned the pages of this marvelous book, I was struck by how little I, a Jewish woman who had gone to Hebrew school for most of her formative years, knew about my religion. In fact, I realized, I didn't have the foggiest idea how to pray.

I started writing down the quotes that interested me the most, facts about the Kabbalah, and the ritual baths, and dybbuks, and the Tree of Life. At the time, I was also writing about a recent trip I had taken to Portugal, and the news I had gotten there of my mother's emergency hysterectomy. I was also writing about my own yoga practice, and the volunteer work I did at a children's hospital in Seattle. As I kept all these windows open in my computer, the voice of the encyclopedia emerged as the binding thread, a way for me to create a spiritual self-portrait in the form of a complex braid.

This is what I love about all braided things: bread, hair, essays, rivers, our own circulatory systems pumping blood to our brains and our hearts. I love the fact of their separate parts intersecting, creating the illusion of wholeness, but with the oh-so-pleasurable texture of separation. It is not the same as a purely disjunctive form, the bits and pieces scattered like cookies on the baking sheet. Rather, the strands are separate, but together, creating a pattern that is lovely to the touch, makes the bread taste even better when we finally lift a slice of it to our tongues.

Poets, of course, have known this all along. They blow the world apart and put it back together again. The collage artist Joseph Cornell wanders the city and is *"lunged into a world of complete happiness in which every triviality becomes imbued with significance . . ."* The poet Charles Simic comments, "The commonplace is miraculous if rightly seen, if recognized."

A BRAIDED HEART

Bread has always been a miracle. As has poetry. And language itself, this tremendous urge to communicate. To live our lives in our shattered ways and still be happy: this is miraculous. The Sabbath bread helps us see that an extraordinary pattern binds our days together. The braided loaf, set on a table, makes of that table an altar. Our hearts may give the illusion of one muscular organ, but think how the florid chambers converge, and of the many veins and arteries that wind their way by design to reach this fleshy core. They come together; they intersect; they beat an urgent rhythm beneath our skin.

MUSIC

I once wrote for a month at an artist's colony in upstate New York, and one of my fellow residents was a composer of operas. He played for us, on the piano, one of his arias. When he was done, we applauded, and I asked him: "How do you know when a piece is finished?" I know now it was a naïve question, even a little foolish.

But he answered me without pause. "When what I hear up here," he said, clasping a palm to his forehead, "corresponds to what's written down here." He pointed to the score. I followed the line of his fingers, saw a page full of inky hieroglyphics that wound in and out of the lined bars.

A writer must spend a great deal of time ushering her piece into the world. There is the creation of bulk, then the cutting down to the essential, resonant notes. This process takes a terrible amount of patience, and more than an inkling of faith. I wanted to spy on that composer through his window and see if he does what *I* do when I'm writing: sitting with a blank stare, my pen poised over the empty page, my mouth hanging slightly ajar, waiting.

When I read the lyric essayists who I consider great, they all have the quality of a piece of music arrived whole from some distant place and played anew. I can go back and read these essays again and again because they seem neither static nor fixed. It's always a live performance: the white space expands and contracts, and I feel like a guest in a charmed province, the same one occupied by prayer.

THE CHALLAH

We pass the bread around the seminar table. I ask my students each to tear off a chunk, and hold it in their hands a moment, waiting until everyone has a piece. I want them to notice the heft of it, the yolky texture, the subtle yet amazing fact that within the loaf itself, once you cut it open, you see nary a sign of the braiding. You have a chunk of bread: whole, fine-grained, delicious.

The bread, of course, is good. All challah is good. And there are many ways to eat it. Some take it apart with their fingers, separating the strands, unwinding them and putting them one by one in their mouths. Some take big bites into the center of the bread, saving the golden crust for last. Some nibble at it, then leave it on their desks. After we're done brushing off the crumbs, taking quick sips of water, we look at each other again.

What I'm hoping is that the idea of *braiding* has entered us, become a viable, perhaps natural, way of shaping our material, and even our lives, for the brief ten weeks we'll be together. What I'm hoping is that by the eating of this bread together we begin to respond to a hunger unsatisfied by everyday food, unvoiced in everyday language. We'll begin to formu-late a few separate strands; we'll mull them over, roll them in our hands, and bring them together in a pattern that acts as a mouthpiece to the sacred.

"Brenda Miller Has a Cold," or:

How a Lyric Essay Happens

It happens like this:

I have a cold. It's what might be termed "a perfect cold," for while my head is stuffed up and my throat tickles (making me cough every six minutes), I'm actually in good spirits, the cotton batting in my head a fine insulation between me and those pesky thoughts that normally pop about in my brain. I can't walk for long without losing my breath, and my muscles ache just enough to make me gravitate toward whatever couch or chair or bed is handy. I can't think very clearly, and my words come out in a voice hoarse and disguised, echoing in my plugged ears. I may be speaking too loudly or too softly—I can't really know, and this person who speaks seems like a separate self, one who is a simpleton, focused only on what is right in front of her: the cup of tea, the box of tissues, a blanket wrapped around her feet. She can see only what happens to flit across her line of vision.

It's a perfect cold, because it just so happens that for this particular week I don't have to do anything but watch the ailment make its way through my body, as it stops to gather a bit of snot here, to drain a bit there. I'm staying on an island in Puget Sound, and I'm with a friend who ferociously writes poetry for ten hours at a time in a room near the water. I can't do much else but sit with a cup of tea in hand, staring at the fireplace or out the window, where I see a mess of deer fence around saplings already so deer-nibbled it's difficult to tell what they're trying to become.

I have a cold, and this means I wake up at odd hours, the night wholly black, and snatches of language float through my brain and stick there, fluttering like any caught prey. In my ordinary body—my clear, unmucoused, narrative life—such fragments glide through continually, but rarely do they sit down and stay, even for a few moments, and lately I bustle right past them even if they do. Instead, my stalwart "to-do" list pulses in the dark, magnetic, drawing me inexorably into its maw.

What I'm trying to say is: *The lyric essay happens when I'm sticky.*

Or it happens like this:

My friend wakes a few minutes after I do, and we say few words to one another, as the day is still dark, and there's coffee to be drunk, and porridge to be shuttled into the mouth, and we're barely aware of one another until I hear her in the shower, and she emerges, fresh and clean and smelling of roses, her briefcase packed, and she wishes me adieu as she swings down the path to her studio. Me—I've barely moved from the couch, into which I keep sinking deeper and deeper, my pajamas warm like a second skin, my eyelids ratcheting back down by increments to the sleep position.

But all this time, the pen stays in my hand, the notebook on my knee, and something is happening; words I can't explain—can't direct, not yet—dump onto the page. I write something like: "... saplings already so deer-nibbled it's difficult to tell what they're trying to become. ..."

What I'm trying to say is: *The lyric essay happens when I've forgotten to get dressed. When I'm disheveled. When I'm not wearing any shoes.*

Or maybe it happens like this:

I've just returned from Michigan, where I probably caught this cold from shaking so many hands in friendly and earnest greeting. There, the women's NCAA basketball tournament was underway, so that many, *many* tall young women wandered the hallways of my hotel, crowding the elevators—stunning in their gray T-shirts and shorts, everything about them declaring *athlete*: their radiant good health, the muscles sleek and toned with practice. They seemed eerily calm in the face of the competition ahead, but then I had no idea who these teams were, or how confident they deserved to be. I couldn't ask, because their beauty made me mute. I pushed the elevator button and nodded at them, got off at my floor without a word.

And what skidded through my brain at the sight of these beautiful women was the way I've always loved basketball—to watch it, mind you, not to play—ever since I was a kid and my brothers played on the backyard court. I love the way action—beautiful, controlled—darts out of what appears to be a chaos of frenzied motion on the court. Bodies seem to sprout limbs more muscled, more gleaming, just all-around more flesh, and then from the morass comes the arc of a steady three-point shot (the shooter can feel it in her hands when she knows it's clean; she turns and trots nonchalantly up court, arms spread wide, shoulders raised in the barest shrug, as if to say: what else did you expect?). . . .

. . . . Or the inside layup—the point guard ferreting out traces of a path through all those bodies that jostle for position under the net, slinking through for the soundless score. . . .

. . . . Or the clean block, all ball, the hand arriving in position at exactly the right moment, the force of it, the surprise. . . .

I knew even then—as a little girl in the L.A. Forum, or shyly watching my brothers from the sidelines in our own backyard—I knew even before I knew the words I'm going to use now: the aesthetic power of instinct coupled with improvisation, of training hitched to transience, the clarity of a plan of action amid a sea of flesh doing its darnedest to make you fail.

Of course, I know now that teams have carefully choreographed plays; they know the strengths and weaknesses of every player on the court. That point guard who just made the impossible layup? She knows the exact moves to make, the quick head-fake, the dribble between the legs, the two-and-a-half steps it would take to lay it up and in. The fall-away reverse jump shot? Practiced hundreds of times. Piece of cake.

But even so: you never know. If all we saw were the practiced drills, the results completely predictable every time (the crowds gathered in the bleachers with their giant "We're Number One" foam fingers and huge plastic tumblers filled with beer), we'd soon grow restless, long before the beer became warm, unappetizing dregs at the bottom of the cup. For much as we love to watch the athletes perform, we don't really want the practiced drill with the predictable outcome. We want the thrill of the unknown, the possibility of utter failure, the exultation of the barest victory, the high fives in the stands . . . the sense that the crowd (the ones who watch) are a part of it all, making it happen with their steadfast attention.

So. Look there, down below, illuminated: the court is a given. The ball, a given. The referees with their shrill whistles, their heavy-footed lumber from one end of the court to the other to make sure there is *some* comportment after all—they, too, are a given, and we hardly note their presence as we shuffle in sideways to our seats. But when those athletes trot onto the floor, that's when it all begins. Expectations rise (literally lift us out of our seats, cheering) and the game begins. From the initial tip of the ball, that first whistle—who knows what will happen next?

What I'm trying to say? *The lyric essay is a three-point shot. It's a desperation thirty-footer. It's a clean steal in the last two seconds of the game.*

I have a cold, which means that at first I get up frequently to fetch the things that surround me—the box of tissues ("specially soft," according to the soothing voice on the box, "made in a special way with soft fibers on the outside and strong fibers on the inside. This gives you the softness you want and the strength you need.") A cup of Breathe Easy tea. A glass of grape juice. A few Advil to stave off the sinus headache lurking in the wings. But in all these forays off the couch, I've never, not even once, looked at myself in the mirror. For someone who usually checks her reflection at every opportunity, this avoidance of my reflection seems peculiar, an aberration. It feels as though—because I have a cold, and because I'm writing so hard, with all I've got—I've become diaphanous.

Transparent. There's nothing really left of me to see.

What this essay is trying to say (ignore for a moment, its author, sitting on the couch, blowing her nose—pay no attention to her, she's getting a little carried away): the lyric essay doesn't look too long at itself in the mirror. It is not "self-reflective," in that it does not really reflect the self who scribbles it down. Rather, it *is* the mirror, the silver film reflecting whatever passes its way. Brenda does not think to look at herself this morning—this morning of the perfect cold—not because she'd rather spare herself the sight of her ugly mug, but because for these few hours she really has no self of which to speak. And that's how the lyric essay happens: when there's no bothersome self to get in the way. When the writing finds its own core. When it finds the language it needs on its own. The lyric essay is *made in a special way with soft fibers on the outside and strong fibers on the inside. This gives you the softness you want and the strength you need.*

So I tell my friend Lee (and I'm lying to her, I'm making it up as I go along): "It's kind of an homage to Gay Talese. To that essay 'Frank Sinatra Has a Cold.'" And she glances at me with that startled, wide-eyed look she gets when she's delighted. I know that "Frank Sinatra Has a Cold" is one of her favorite essays of all time, and that's another reason I've made up this half-truth, to give some pleasure, to have this fleeting connection.

"Really?" she says. "Do *you* at least show up?"

In the Gay Talese profile, made famous on its publication in *Esquire* in 1966, Frank Sinatra has a cold. Which changes everything. The narrative shifts. Expectations shuffle and scuttle and get out of the way. The interview Talese was after? Gone. Sinatra never even looks at him. Sinatra's in a bad mood. The songs now will be difficult to sing. Not as polished. Not as rehearsed. Sinatra can't stand it. It feels as though the cold will last forever, that his voice will never be the same.

Talese hangs around anyway. Takes notes on all the things surrounding Sinatra, his ostensible subject. The notebook from his research is a thing of beauty, itself a piece of art, with doodles and arrows and words spilling across the margins. Nothing stays in place, but even through the scribble we see a structure emerge, a sense of direction: SCENE TWO, he writes in big block letters, surrounded by asterisks. ACT ONE. He watches Sinatra's character emerge, gain complexity, through his inter-actions with others. Sees him blow up over a pair of boots that Harlan Ellison wears at a club. Sees him smile at a woman in the crosswalk, disarming her completely, and then disappear. Sinatra's at the center, but we can't access him directly. He shows up, but only in flashes, only in transit. We have to sit on a barstool a few feet away, just watching to see what might be revealed.

Do *I* show up? Sometimes I do, and sometimes I don't.

You try to tell a simple story, walk a simple path, but keep losing sight of your destination. The destination is no longer as interesting as the diversions. You hear a wren sing so loudly inside the deer fence, and she startles you, and then you see her, how easily she slips though that cage *around saplings already so deer-nibbled it's difficult to tell what they're try-ing to become.* You are just trying to become. No, not trying. Trying is too trying. You're just becoming.

Anyway, you have a cold, so you're not going to walk too far. You'll sit down for frequent rests, just to catch your breath. Your breath will fas-cinate you, become something you can no longer take for granted, the rhythm of it: in . . . out . . . and then the slightest pause before you feel it again: the body's insistence on keeping you alive.

What I'm trying to say is: *the lyric essay happens in the gaps. In the pause before the next breath demands to be taken.*

So here's the deal:

You have a cold, and then you don't. Gradually you get better. Or you get worse, and then you get better. Rarely does anyone die of a head cold.

Sometimes you notice you're getting better, and sometimes you don't. Sometimes you just wake up one day and realize you haven't coughed all night, that you have not one crumpled, sticky tissue lying next to your bed. Your body has been returned, intact and clear.

And your self? You can, if you so desire, now go to Point B from Point A with a brisk, direct stride, hardly pausing, undistracted by the scenery. You can go to work, and be your work-a-day self; you can be productive as all get-out. When people ask how you are, you can say "I'm fine" without lying. You can tell the truth, the unvarnished truth, no half-truths, no need to make anything up just for the heck of it. Well, that's *good*, people will say, I'm glad you're feeling *better*, and you'll nod in agreement, but some part of you, some part that's not fit for civilized company, wonders if this self—this clear, narrative, undeterred self—really is *good*, really is *better*. Some part of you longs to be sick again—not *sick* sick, just enough so you can be buffered a little while longer, not quite so direct and so clear.

The poet Mark Doty says it happens like this: *Grace might descend in its odd, circuitous routes. We are visited by joy, seem to be given a poem or a song, something we encounter fills us to the rim of the self. Those things point the way, but who lives in that heightened state of awareness?*

In Michigan—amid the basketball players and the spring rains—protestors clog the streets with signs, commemorating the fourth anniversary of the Iraq war. They only want us to notice. Just notice. And to remember, even before that, the bombing of Afghanistan.

So I oblige. I'm an obliging person. I remember a large hall, with red-planked floors. Candlelight. A scattering of people sitting on *zafus* and *zabutons*, waiting for a bell, a bell that sits in front of me, waiting to be struck. Then someone hands me a slip of paper, and I nod, like a judge whose just been apprised of the verdict. I deliberately set the piece of paper aside on my cushion, all eyes now on me, expectant, and I know, fleetingly, what it means to age: to have a snippet of knowledge a split second before someone else, to have the power to impart this knowledge or not, and the passing of this knowledge through you, leaving its trace.

I nod, and I look at the people gathered here in a circle, these people who have come to a meditation hall on a Wednesday evening with no particular agenda in mind but to practice breathing in and breathing out, to observe how predictably the mind will wander from that simple task to more complicated things. "They have started dropping bombs in Afghanistan," I say, and a dozen heads nod, as if we know what is meant by *they*, as if we know what is meant by *bombs*, as if we know *Afghanistan*. As if we know what to do with such knowledge now that it has become ours.

But they are only words on a piece of paper. I set it aside. I ring a little bell. We sit and breathe in and out—some of us, I'm sure, thinking (trying not to think) of Afghani children, of what happens to a body when it's dismembered. We know something has happened. But we don't really know. All we can do is imagine. All we can do is try to put the pieces together in a way that makes sense.

What I'm trying to say is: In the lyric essay, it all shows up. The good and the bad—they jostle one another, rub shoulders, emit sparks. The stuff we try to remember, and the stuff that remembers itself.

The lyric essay . . . *it's happening.*

That's all I'm trying to say. It's *a* happening, like those hippie gatherings I dreamt of as a teenager as I walked to Patrick Henry Junior High, the suburban streets so calm, so predictable. Somewhere to the north of us, students burned the star-spangled banner, singing anthems that bore no resemblance to the patriotic hymn we belted out on the playground. In the streets of San Francisco, young men and women danced in circles, smiling at one another, *loving the one you're with.* They dropped acid and smoked pot and heard the *doors of perception* clatter open in their brains.

But we—my classmates and I—we lived in the suburbs of Los Angeles where life proceeded in routines so smooth we barely noticed them. Our parents did not get divorced, our houses did not fall apart, even in the occasional earthquake that rocked the town.

And then I read *Electric Kool-Aid Acid Test* three times in a row, and I wanted nothing more than to attend a *happening*. A *happening* would change me forever. I imagined a large warehouse filled with beautiful people dancing their hearts out, breathing hard, doing strange and wondrous things to one another. The great thing about *happenings* was the way they just happened. No one planned them. No one knew what to expect.

You bring together a few elements as givens: A big empty space, some musicians prone to improvisation, a few substances geared to short-circuit one's capacity to make logical, streamlined narratives. But that's it. The rest is up to you. Well, not *you*, exactly, because there is no longer a solid concept of you, a you that has any true agency or control.

And who knows what might be alchemized in this mix? Maybe someone will make balloon animals, his breath huffing to bring them to life, squeaking them into the shapes of deer and foxes and wrens that really take flight. Maybe two someones will make love in the dark; one of them might have a cold, and the kisses will make her wheeze, but this will not diminish the force of her desire. A basketball game might erupt on the floor, or a Hula-Hoop contest, or Frisbees might float weightless, suspended in the air. Maybe Sinatra will show up, crooning love songs, beaming his bright blue eyes to make us swoon. Maybe two giant puppets will lurch toward the stage, cradling the war dead in their arms.

The poet Paisley Rekdal says: *I suppose it is an accident anything is beautiful.*

But whatever happens, surely we'll dance. Heads bopping, arms swinging, sweat glazing our backs. A feral dance—one that makes itself up as it goes along. That's the only thing we can know for sure.

A Case Against Courage in Creative Nonfiction

Recently I gave a reading of a personal essay that was, well, *really* personal; it inadvertently revealed more about myself than I'd intended. Alas, this happens quite frequently: while I'm actually shy and quiet in my "real" life, put paper and pen in front of me and I'll say anything, blurt out the most intimate details with no coercion whatsoever. I must be in a kind of trance when I do this, unaware of the real import of what I'm doing; I must be, as Cynthia Ozick has put it, in thrall to the "ghost writer" at work. In her essay "Ghost Writers," she says, "Writers are what they genuinely are only when they are at work in the silent and instinctual cell of ghostly solitude and never when they are out industrially chatting on the terrace."

When I give a reading, I'm "chatting on the terrace," but I've forgotten to put my clothes on before venturing out in public. I've been following instinct with my eyes closed, not primping in front of a mirror, so I'll blithely get up in front of a crowd of strangers and read what was conceived in the dark, concentrating only on the words and sentences and sounds, surprised, when I look up, to see embarrassed smirks on faces in the audience.

After this particular reading, people came up to congratulate me on the piece. Some zoomed right in and shook my hand; some hung back a little, embarrassed, whispering together. Most of them looked me up and down, as if appraising me in a new light. And all of them used the word "brave." As in: *you were so brave to read that essay.* Or *what a brave piece!* Or, the one that really made me wince, whispered as a confidence in my ear: *I could never be brave enough to write something like that.*

I thanked everyone warmly, and I really did appreciate their praise, but I went back to my seat feeling suddenly self-conscious, deflated, a fraud. Brave? I'm afraid of my own shadow. And to anoint me as *brave* made me feel as if I had really done something wrong, something no one in their right mind would do: risk making an ass of myself in public. Bravery implied that I had screwed up my courage to both write and read that essay, when courage had nothing to do with it. I had simply been in my chair writing. I had been following form and language and voice to get the essay where it wanted to go; at some point momentum had taken over. I didn't even know what I was writing until I'd written it, and I'd been chuckling the whole time, enjoying myself immensely. I'd read the piece only because I liked the form so much, loved reading that voice aloud. *Brave?* Uh-oh, I thought, what have I done?

The words "brave" and "courage" seem to come up with great frequency when we read creative nonfiction work that reveals intimate details about an author's life. We see the acclamation "a brave memoir" in book reviews, or find the adjective "courageous" popping up among the cover blurbs. We overhear the whispers, "how brave," at a reading where both the writer and the audience have found themselves near tears.

But is it really bravery we're witnessing? And is courage now considered part of the basic skill set of the autobiographical writer? In fact, I wonder if distilling strong emotion into images and voices that will endure actually takes the *opposite* of courage. What does it take? Maybe a certain naiveté. Denial that we are doing anything dangerous. Perhaps it actually takes courage's evil twin, cowardice—a refusal to really face those emotions the way a normal, healthy person would, retreating instead into the refuge of form: words, sentences, images. Maybe it really takes avarice, a desire to plunder the most exposed parts of the self for the sake of a good paragraph.

I have great respect and admiration for writers who are willing to risk something in their work; as we all know, powerful writing must risk something in one way or another. And it can certainly be daunting to speak when silence is so much more comfortable. But I've come to see that at some point—some crucial point—we need to shift our allegiance from experience itself, to the *artifact* we're making of that experience on the page. To do so, we mustn't find courage; we must, instead, become keenly interested in metaphor, image, syntax, and structure: all the stuff that comprises *form*. We are hammering out parallel plot lines, not plumbing the depths of our souls, but as a collateral to that technical work the soul does indeed get tapped and gushes forth.

This allegiance to artifact over experience perhaps becomes most obvious when we experience nonfiction in lyric forms. When creative nonfiction writers choose to write in nonlinear forms such as the short-short essay, the braided essay, or the "hermit crab" (a term I coined in the first edition of *Tell It Slant: Writing and Shaping Creative Nonfiction* for an essay that appropriates an already existing form to tell its story), they magnify the fact that they are manipulating experience for the sake of art. These writers immediately signal to the reader that the intent is not necessarily to convey information or fact, or to bravely illuminate dark areas of one's life, but to create the truth of literature, of metaphor—a truth that is not always so direct.

Case in point: that really personal essay I read in public? I wrote it in the most impersonal form: a "table of figures," where the personal narrative is told, and embedded within, the ostensibly descriptive voice of an objective list of contents: i.e.: "Figure 1.1: A girl becomes aware of herself as a girl. . . ." By contrasting deeply interior material with the more public persona, I mitigated any sense that I might be about to perform an act of indecent exposure in public.

Once we start writing, in whatever form (including traditional narratives), experience instantly becomes transmuted into artifact, whose close cousin is "artifice." In lyric essays, this sense of artifice becomes magnified—the forms often draw attention to themselves, and so the fact that one is creating an artifact, not a transcript of experience, becomes more obvious. There are gaps, moments of silence, other voices, and/or a magnification of a single moment in time: all these techniques signal to a reader that we're in a realm where there is no absolute truth, where imagination will come into play, where experience is quite obviously being shaped for literary or artistic purposes.

For some writers, especially beginning writers, the conscious use of form can sometimes be the only way certain kinds of truths can be approached at all. Since these truths need to be contained more forcefully, form essentially *becomes* the writer's inky courage, much the way the use of form in poetry can give rise to astonishing work. As poetry teachers often witness, when a student's mind is engaged with the rules of a villanelle or a sestina, the most creative and heartfelt content often arises, the "bravest" content.

Concrete forms allow for what I like to call "inadvertent revelations," where the writer no longer seems in complete control. Revelation, or discovery, emerges organically from the writing; the *essay* now seems to reveal information about the writer, rather than the writer revealing these tidbits directly to the reader. In the lyric essay class I teach, I often start with an essay from Stephen Dunn; it is one line long, with the title "Little Essay on Form": "We build the corral as we reinvent the horse." This "little essay" automatically sets up the synergy that exists between form and content, and this little manifesto insists that content may dictate form as surely as form can shape content.

We then go on to experiment with form: first the short-shorts, where the restricted space of a single page encourages students to magnify *small* details until they yield meaning. There's little room for abstract thought or cliché or long-winded setups in the short-short form—no runway on which to build up one's courage—and so experience is shaped to give precedence to image, scene, detail, subtle metaphor, not necessarily to "feelings" or bare emotion. We use the online journal *Brevity*, edited by Dinty W. Moore, to seek out models for this form. In one such essay, "The Sloth," by Jill Christman, we see that the impetus for writing may have its roots in deep and scary emotion, but the writing goes beyond that, finds the mettle to explore this emotion through keen observation, precise language, and organic metaphor. It begins:

There is a nothingness of temperature, a point on the body's mercury where our blood feels neither hot nor cold. I remember a morning swim on the black sand eastern coast of Costa Rica four months after my twenty-two-year-old fiancé was killed in a car accident. Walking into the water, disembodied by grief, I felt no barriers between my skin, the air, and the water.

Later, standing under a trickle of water in the wooden outdoor shower, I heard a rustle, almost soundless, and looking up, expecting something small, I saw my first three-toed sloth.

Notice how Christman's description of grief is not so much an emotional feeling as a physical one: "no barriers between my skin, the air, and the water." She gives us the context for this situation quickly—a fiancé killed—but her most effective move is that *she does not start with that line*. No, we start with a fact external to her own experience, a physical fact that will become the focal point for Christman's overarching metaphor. With this ostensibly simple move, Christman shows us that she has the perspective to translate experience into artifact, and she is not screwing up her courage so much as becoming keenly interested in the connections between her own inner state of mind and the images the outer world provides her. Noticing the sloth, the narrator takes herself out of introspection and so, in the end, this story becomes not a polemic about her own personal grief, but about new insights into the *nature* of grief, an articulation that does not necessarily arise from one's own experience, but from a literary reimagining of that experience:

I thought I knew slow, but this guy, this guy was *slow*. The sound I heard was his wiry-haired blond elbow, brushed green with living algae, stirring a leaf as he reached for the next branch. Pressing my wet palms onto the rough wooden walls, I watched the sloth move in the shadows of the canopy. Still reaching. And then still reaching.

What else is this slow? Those famous creatures of slow—the snail, the tortoise—they move faster. Much. This slow seemed impossible, not real, like a trick of my sad head. Dripping and naked in the jungle, I thought, *That sloth is as slow as grief.* We were numb to the speed of the world. We were one temperature.

These paragraphs end the short essay. From a statement of fact about an equilibrium of temperature, we come full circle, but this fact is now imbued with much more meaning. Because the essay is so short, every image must be precise, every word must further the narrator's discovery in a focused and measured way. The essay must move like the sloth—slowly, deliberately—opening up space for this grief to manifest in the reader's own heart. Christman didn't need courage; she needed that sloth. She needed that sloth to carry the weight of her grief for her, and eventually for us.

In my class, we then go on to the collage essay and its cousin, the braided essay, where students begin to expand this emphasis on scene and detail and experiment with connecting disparate strands of thought together. We use Abigail Thomas's *Safekeeping* as a model of this technique; she experiments with point of view, gaps in information, short vignettes, and direct address. The book is riddled with white space (some of the chapters are only a line or two long), and the white space becomes a voice all its own, allows room for the reader to interact with the images and the material she offers us, to create something new all over again.

For example, the entire second "chapter" of *Safekeeping*, titled "Offering," is one single paragraph, set in the middle of the page:

> While you were alive the past was a live unfinished thing. Like a painting we weren't done with. Like a garden we were still learning to tend. Nothing was set in stone yet, and weren't we ourselves still changing? We might redeem our past by redeeming ourselves. I had in mind a sort of alchemy. But then you died, and just like that, it was over. What was done was done. Now we could never fix it. All I can do is chip away, see what comes off in my hand, look for a shape.

The book unfolds from this initial offering; it acts as a compact between narrator and reader that we are not going to simply narrate a difficult experience, but that we will be "chipping away" at it, and the book's form will necessarily mirror this intent. We, the readers, peer over her shoulder as the bits and pieces assemble themselves into a story of complicated love and grief. She exposes all kinds of information about herself, about her husband and her ex-husbands, but throughout it all we feel the way the form keeps her covered. She is taking things one bit at a time. The book gently encourages her to be honest, to keep telling the truth.

Thomas also engages two allies in this endeavor: her second husband, who has just died, and to whom she directs much of this narrative; and her sister, who speaks up to help Thomas clarify the story, at moments in the narrative when it may become overwhelming. The second husband provides the intimate sounding board for these stories—he provides the context, the reason, for this deep examination. Thomas directs her first words not to the reader, but to this ex-husband: "I am remembering this time just before I knew you and then I knew you, and then you died. It makes the parentheses within which I lived most of my life. Not knowing you, knowing you, and then you died. Twenty-seven years. A long time." By considering this period of her life as a "parentheses," Thomas automatically contains it, makes it manageable. And by evoking that image of the parentheses at the very beginning, she sets a tone that is, itself, "parenthetical;" the meditations, scenes, and memories that make up this work have the tone of undercurrent, the story that is "inside," within, or murmured as an aside to the official narrative.

The narrator's sister keeps her honest; she acts as a Greek chorus encouraging Thomas to look at all sides of the story, and to look at it from an outsider's perspective. She allows Thomas to explore more directly (or indirectly, for it becomes an overheard conversation) some of the key issues of this autobiographical narrative. For example:

> There are already a lot of husbands floating around, my sister says.
>
> Well yes, I say. I married three times.
>
> That's what I'm saying. A lot of husbands. Somebody's going to get confused. Maybe even annoyed.

Or, later in the book:

Where are the kids? my sister wants to know.

I can't write about the kids, I say uneasily.

But they are a part of this, she says. Their lives.

Their lives are their own, I say. . . .

They should be here.

But they are everywhere, I say, they are on every page. Don't you see?

See what?

They are the whole point.

By linking up with these allies, Thomas need not muster up her own courage. She has, instead, found refuge in literary technique, in form, in metaphor. Even the book's title, *Safekeeping*, and the cover image on the original paperback edition—a glass canning jar filled with scraps of paper—implies the kind of refuge one can find in form. In the eponymous chapter, she narrates a story her mother told her, about a time in the mountains of Switzerland when her parents came upon an ancient church: "It was late afternoon, getting toward dusk, and as they began to walk away, my mother said all of a sudden they could hear the disembodied voices of nuns coming through the windows of the church singing the same song they had sung at the same hour every day for the last five hundred years. 'If safekeeping has a sound,' she said, 'then surely this was it.'"

Safekeeping happens in the rituals, the forms that have been in use for hundreds of years. Once we find the right voice, sometimes a voice bolstered by the ones who have come before us, courage is no longer the one necessary trait keeping us on track. Through enacting the practiced ritual of writing—writing with verve and focus and skill—we keep ourselves safe, and we keep our stories safe, and we extend this sanctuary to others.

As my students read *Safekeeping*, I can see their faces relax. Where once they were tight, afraid, resistant, suddenly they understand the grace of the small snippet. They are absolved from having to tell the whole story at once. They are allowed moments of silence to recuperate. And they produce astonishing work. I've had students write about sensitive topics—such as living with a mother who has unmedicated bipolar disorder, or the suicide of a friend—quite successfully, because they no longer rely only on their courage to get this story out. They begin to understand how form allows them to contain experience in sturdy jars, to find its most salient boundaries. As the memoirist Bernard Cooper has said: "Only when the infinite has edges am I capable of making art."

The braided essay, while closely allied with collage, offers a slightly different form of armor when venturing into dangerous or risky material. In these essays, strands form, disappear, and reappear at strategic moments, creating a lively, interactive structure in which one's personal material now can find the way its threads interweave with material the world offers. The personal and the more "impersonal" can play off one another to create new meaning.

In Sherry Simpson's essay, "Fidelity," for example, she begins an emotionally wrenching piece about the complexities of marriage not with a scene of that marriage—the fights, the doubts, the ambivalence—but with a bear:

> I saw the bear first. I turned from the ocean's calm edge toward the dusky blue of Reid Glacier, and there it was, striding over the spit in the honeyed evening light, stiff green stalks of beach rye parting against its flanks. The bear was coming toward us. It was looking at us.
>
> "There's a bear," I said. My voice was low. My husband was standing by the kayak and turned around to look. I did not know what else to say.

In this vivid first scene, we readers do not yet know what territory we'll be heading into (though the title gives us a good clue, plants the theme in our consciousness); we're simply hooked to know what will happen with that bear. As the essay progresses, Simpson interrupts this scene repeatedly to play it against the narrative strand of her marriage, so that it quickly becomes clear that this one vivid, extended scene with the bear—and the way husband and wife must face this danger together, the different ways they face this danger together—becomes emblematic of marriage itself. In that first section all the themes are planted for the essay to come: the lurking presence of danger, the impossibility

that words will ward off that danger, the different directions these part-
ners face, and how eventually they reconcile those differences to work
together in order to survive.

The scene with the bear becomes what I like to call a "container"
scene; not only does it provide narrative momentum (we want to know
what physically happens), it "contains" the strong emotions involved in
dealing with sensitive, emotional material. We come back to the bear
four times in the narrative, and in between Simpson gives us scenes from
the marriage, difficult scenes rendered quickly, with just the right detail.
For example: "One night in bed, thinking of all I'd been learning without
him, I said, *You're a speed bump in my life.* It may have been the cruelest
thing I've ever said. He looked at me and replied, *I love you with all my
heart. Why isn't that enough?* I couldn't say, but I knew the failure was in
me, in wanting to make him something he was not and never would be."

These reflections on her own culpability, the portrayal of the husband
with his vulnerabilities and flaws, and her gradual insight into the essential nature of this relationship are all subsumed in the context of this
one bear who seems to keep stalking the couple on this trip through
the wilderness. The bear provides the narrator with an outer, concrete
image that both bolsters and buffers the emotional material to come.
The narrator and her husband, once they shake the bear, end up in an
easy camaraderie, having survived both ordeals—bear and marriage:

> Such a relief to be still and quiet, to lie there open to the world and returned
> to ourselves. I slept with one hand tucked into his sleeping bag, one palm
> pressed against that steady warmth. In the morning, we sat and watched
> the clear light fill the stormy basin, grateful that for once there was nothing
> more to say.

I know it can seem a paradox: that writings imbued with qualities
that we recognize as "honest" or "brave" may actually be so strong
because they focus *away* from that material directly. This refocus can be
on form, yes, but can also zero in on details that exist at an oblique slant
to the center of the piece, such as that bear. These essays employ what
I call "peripheral vision": turning the gaze to focus on something that
seems peripheral to the emotional center or ostensible topic. Instead of

facing your "stuff" head on, you turn away from it, zero in on something that has fluttered up on the side, and see what angle it gives you. In this way we sidle up to the real material and actually find new meaning in it—artistic meaning.

My students and I move on from collage and braided essays to experiment with the "hermit crab" essay; in these essays, sensitive material finds a carapace outside of the self. Such essays can take the form of a "how to" article, for instance, or a "to do" list, or a menu, or a field guide. For example, one student had been trying for months to write about her experience growing up with a mother who had hoarding disorder; her home was a nightmare, and the first drafts I saw were incoherent, long rambles without any center. When she chose to write this material in the form of a real-estate ad ("Home for Sale"), the voice became crystal clear, the images indelible and coherent. The "I" was taken out of it; the narrator now became the "owner's daughter" who reports on the condition of the home. As the chirpy voice of the real estate ad—meant to extol the virtues of a property—finds itself instead detailing items such as scores of broken dolls, sacks of buttons, last year's newspapers, bags of garbage creating seven-foot walls around the room, the reader puts the picture together and seems to experience it, paradoxically, *more* directly, seemingly without intervention from the narrator. The discord between the intent of a real estate ad (which lies and covers up defects in houses) and the intent of this essay (to reveal *all* the defects, both physically and emotionally) automatically creates meaning and gave my student the distance (the courage?) she needed to clearly see the experience herself.

Another student thought she wanted to explore her proclivity for true-crime novels, and she did so in the form of a crossword puzzle, complete with clues that the reader is invited to try to answer herself. But what emerges, inadvertently, is also this woman's abusive childhood, which may or may not have led her to this fascination with "true crime." She leaves some of the spaces on this puzzle deliberately blank, because sometimes there are no easy answers.

Hermit crabs are vulnerable creatures who find an alien, empty shell to inhabit as their own—to protect their soft underbellies. When you're crawling around in a beautiful shell, there's really not that much to be afraid of. You don't need courage anymore, because you're protected by something outside the self. In fact, you can really start enjoying the view.

In all these cases, my students naturally needed courage and fortitude to deal with this material in their own lives, but in the *writing itself*, courage was not the key factor in the piece's success. Once they are writing these essays, my students often use the words "fun," or "easy," or "exciting": not words we usually associate with dangerous and courageous ordeals. And the resulting work has the qualities of playfulness that allow us to enter these dangerous worlds fully open to whatever will be revealed, now more fully equipped to render these insights into strong writing.

I served as the editor-in-chief of *Bellingham Review* for thirteen years, and I was always drawn to writing that contains this kind of self-awareness about voice and form. We run the Annie Dillard Award for Creative Nonfiction, and when I was editor we'd often receive about 400 manuscripts. My editors and I dove into the piles of anonymous submissions, eager to find the voices that would make themselves heard in the crowd. In this harsh, survival-of-the-fittest environment, almost every topic can seem old hat; it's the voice that matters. Voice and form. When we came across writers who mastered the art of signaling that their allegiance is firmly on the side of artifact over experience, that's an author we'd be willing to follow anywhere.

So, picture this: my weary nonfiction editors and I are sitting in my living room, remnants of cold pizza scattered on the coffee table, dregs of coffee filming over in the coffee cups. Sheaves of white paper tumble everywhere, paper clips litter every surface, and our minds have gone a little numb. We're giving everything the "two-minute" glance: if the piece makes a fatal error in the first page, it will probably not receive a second look. If it bores us, it will drift over into the reject pile.

And, unfortunately, most of these pieces announce themselves as yet another rendition of "this happened to me, I'm being brave, please listen." This earnestness makes us sigh and turn to the next piece in the stack. We don't really want to hear what happened to this stranger. But if that's the case, what are we doing reading these stacks and stacks of nonfiction? What is it we *want?*

Then, something catches our eye. A first paragraph like: "Once every six months or so, when she was thirteen or fourteen, my sister would wash her trumpet. It was never announced; in fact, I only came upon it by accident. . . . I noticed her kneeling by the tub, leaning out of view, as I walked down our hall, and slipped into the bathroom to investigate."

A trumpet. A bathtub. A narrator who goes to investigate this congruence of two incongruent things. And here, in just a few lines, we feel the unmistakable tingle of what, for us, makes a piece of creative nonfiction "literature of palpable quality" (our journal's motto, our rallying cry). The narrator does not force us to gaze upon her life and her experience; rather, she *invites* us to look with her at the common things that both startle and amaze.

This essay, titled "Subimago," goes on, in a fragmented gait, to explore not only trumpets and sisters and things that are washed, but mayflies and bodies and the inevitability of change. After not too long a time, we return to that trumpet and that bathtub and that sister, with an ending that begins: "The afternoon when I caught my sister washing her trumpet, I had taken two steps from the hall, leaned forward, leaned back, and in those few seconds seen transformed too many things: the trumpet as an organism, with valves refracted by water that bent from right to left as easily as arms and legs, and my sister as mother, bending over the tub; she would in fact be washing her own child before I was as old as she was at the time. But perhaps what was most incredulous of all was that in that room, at that moment, in spite of the trumpet, there was no possibility of music."

And so this piece, by Jill Sisson Quinn, happily goes into the finalist pile, and then is picked as the first-place winner for 2003 by judge Kim Barnes, who in her comments described it this way: "Magical in its telling and transcendent in its tone, 'Subimago' is an examination of narrative truth and how that truth can shift and redefine our sense of ourselves and those around us."

Now, when I look at Quinn's piece, and the judge's comments, again, I realize that this is essentially what happens when we read for the contest; among all the faceless voices, only those emerge that are "magical and transcendent" either in voice or form, and these pieces usually focus not only on their content, but on the nature of storytelling itself.

Mark Doty puts it better. "An unshaped utterance is not a poem," he says to Bill Moyers in an interview for the book *Fooling with Words*:

> We shape a poem in order to let it go; the process of crafting the poem, of trying to get everything from line to sonic texture to each individual word just right involves standing back and gaining a greater degree of distance from what we've said. A good poem may begin in self expression, but it ends as art, which means it isn't really for the writer anymore, but for the reader who steps into and makes the experience of the poem her or his own.

Substitute "essay" for "poem" and you have a good idea of what I'm arguing. He doesn't say that courage is needed to make a powerful piece. As artists what we need is a laser-bright eye. We need dispassion. We need to find our way using all the precision tools at our disposal: image, diction, syntax, and form.

One author, for me, exemplifies this stance quite well. In his memoir *Truth Serum*, Bernard Cooper reveals all kinds of things one might feel a little reticent about bringing up in public. He describes, in stunning detail and scene, his experiences growing up as a gay boy in Los Angeles, coming to terms with his sexuality, and then living as a gay man in the era of AIDS. The writing is sometimes whimsical, always elegant, with a keen ear for just the right syntax and sounds. In the longer essays, his narrative structures are architecturally complex; my students and I often spend hours mapping out the through-line of his plots, the way he can hang both past and future on an anchoring thread that propels the essay from beginning to end.

In his eponymous essay "Truth Serum," for example, a visit to his therapist's office (where he is seeking a "cure" for his homosexuality), becomes the through-line for an essay that goes back in time to his first sexual experiences with women, up to the present moment when he is living with a woman, and into the future, when he will settle into his identity as a gay man. Throughout it all, we periodically return to the doctor's office, where the narrator is compelled to tell the truth through the injection of truth serum. The onset of this drug leads to some pleasant physical sensations:

> I barely felt the injection, but serum rode into my vein like an intravenous hot toddy, and a primal comfort seemed to radiate outward from the tip of the needle. Almost instantly, I began to take in rich, intoxicating breaths of air. I steeped in a heedless stew of sensation: felt the rubber release from my arm; heard small talk volley between the doctors; saw shiny fronds of philodendron, which seemed like the greenest things on earth. With the sudden candor of a drunk, I wanted to tell the doctors how happy I felt, but before the words could form, I heard what I thought was a receptionist typing in another room. Her typing would quicken—faster, manic, superhuman—and invariably I would think to myself: A million words a minute! What nimble fingers! The keys must be shooting sparks from the friction! And then I'd realize it wasn't the sound of typing after all, but something more miraculous— chattering watts of light showered down from a bulb on the ceiling. Stirred to the verge of tears, I wanted to shout, "Hold everything doctors. I can hear light!"

The serum amplifies everything, sets his senses on high, and in the aftermath of the initial rush he is supposed to be able to express his essential truths. He will have the "sudden candor of a drunk." Throughout the essay, this "candor" reappears again and again, as Cooper honestly explores his sexual feelings, coming to a conclusion that will disappoint his doctors but be the launch pad for the rest of his life.

The doctor's office becomes the anchoring point of this complex narrative, a supposedly safe place where he is encouraged to plumb the inner depths; it becomes a suspended moment outside the flow of everyday life when the narrator can reflect on the experience with the benefit of hindsight. Later in the essay we return to the doctor's office, where Cooper muses, "I suppose I understood that no behavioral modification, no psychological revelation, was going to take away my desire for men, but in the end I went back to Dr. Sward's office because—this is the hardest confession of all—I wanted to hear the light."

In a book full of hard confessions, this may seem like a trivial one: this lust for heightened sensation, for supernatural energy, for a view of the world that overwhelms our deepest shame. But it's exactly the articulation of this confession that shows us that this writer has a handle on his experience, that he's employing peripheral vision to get us to the heart of the matter in an artistic way. The real "truth serum" in this essay is the writing itself, a prose that goes beyond the "facts" and gets at a truth accessed only through this artistic interpretation of experience. This serum gets injected into one's veins the moment potent words start coalescing into sentences, sentences that please us, that create their own rhythm. Truth serum activates when we find the right voice, the right form; when we've practiced enough that we can tell when we're onto something. We "hear the light." We become candid as drunks. This truth serum loosens our lips, discretion be damned.

In his essay "Marketing Memory," Cooper expresses his befuddlement at the reaction to his prose. Of course, he responds with pleasure at praise, but he tells us:

> After a reading, people would sometimes commend me for my "honesty" and "courage" in writing about sexuality. . . . I thanked these people, but tried to explain that I felt neither honest nor brave when I worked with personal subjects because the rigors of shaping sentences and paragraphs overwhelmed any sense that I was dealing with risky or revealing subject matter. In the end, my history became so much raw material to temper in the forge of craft. . . . Since "honesty" in writing is so often artless and indulgent, and since mere audacity so often masquerades as "courage," I was actually a little bothered by the suggestion that these were the work's most notable qualities. I'd hoped that the formal aspects of my autobiographical writing—its structure, language, and juxtaposition of images—were what made it worthwhile.

Honesty, authenticity, bravery: all these qualities emerge under cover of form, voice, metaphor, syntax. We have our fears, certainly, and our deep emotions, but the brave writer is one who comes to care more about words, sentences, and the careful construction of scene than about the feelings or experiences that engendered these words in the first place. These writers understand the ways that artifact owes a debt to experience, but that experience itself no longer has the upper hand.

Writing Inside the Web:

Creative Nonfiction in the Age of Connection

FREE BOX

The Free Box always stood on the front porch of the lodge, its heavy lid growing soft at the edges from so many hands lifting and peering in. A Free Box lures you, no matter what else you might be doing at the time. A Free Box is a promise. A Free Box is not a box that is free (though sometimes I did want to cart away the box itself, to have this treasure chest hidden away in my cottage); it's the contents inside that are ready to be given away.

The Free Box I'm remembering lived at Orr Hot Springs in northern California, in the early 80s—an era that believed the universe provided gifts if one knew the right way to ask. The lodge, filled with ratty couches and heavy wood dining tables, hunkered down in the center of the community; from the front porch you could watch naked people ambling their way toward the baths. You could watch the herb garden flowering, or eavesdrop on romances that kindled or faded on the front lawn. You could watch the light shift over the cliffs that loomed above, and spot red-tailed hawks circling in the updrafts. You could hear pots and pans clanking in the kitchen as people made their communal meals, hair still damp from the sauna. Over it all: the hiss of sulfur from underground, the smell of mineralized steam.[1]

You never knew what you might find in the Free Box—usually tattered concert T-shirts, but sometimes something unusually lovely might catch your eye: a tie-dyed scarf, a crocheted shawl, a porcelain teacup with a chipped handle. We never saw anyone actually put anything *in* the Free Box, yet it always seemed full. We often did see people standing in that posture peculiar to someone foraging for the unexpected: one hand holding the lid up, the other sifting through the items as if panning for gold—head bent, eyes intent: the forager wanted to appear disinterested, casual, but the studious tilt of the head gave away the seriousness of this search.

There might be a pair of rainbow suspenders, or a half-empty bottle of olive oil. There might be Birkenstocks worn down at the heel. There might be a long dress with lace at the hem, or a swollen, waterlogged book of poems by Kahlil Gibran, his words now smudged, but still earnest: *To you the earth yields her fruit, and you shall not want if you but know how to fill your hands. It is in exchanging the gifts of the earth that you shall find abundance and be satisfied.*[2]

These were castoffs, yes, but at the time they did not feel like castoffs to us, but gifts simply waiting for a home. Or not gifts, exactly, but artifacts of other lives, looking to tell a story. Or not a story, exactly, but a fragment of the web that connects one human being to the next.

---

1 Here's where, if I turned my Wi-Fi connection on, I would probably start moseying around websites looking for information about hot springs, the composition of minerals, etc., but I've turned off the internet in order to concentrate. Because I know that bit of research would lead me to the shopping sites where I need to buy some stuff for my new hot tub in the backyard. And I need to call the guy about the bamboo hedge, and maybe I should get some fertilizer for the bamboo I already have. Etc. Etc.

2 Okay, so yes, you caught me: I had no Kahlil Gibran memorized, so I clicked on the Wi-Fi for *just a minute* to look it up, and lo, it was good: within thirty seconds I had lines from a poem that so perfectly connect to the theme this essay is developing it brings tears to my eyes. Now I can smugly let those lines stand like sentinels at the end of the paragraph, waving their beacons. And now that I have those lines, the essay has moved from embryo to fetus stage and I understand where I'm going. Now I can get up, make another cup of coffee, look outside at the rain, think about taking a soak in the hot tub, then sit back down again. I'll think about looking at my email since the Wi-Fi is back on. And I do. And I send some emails. Okay, now I'm back.

When we put on those suspenders, or slipped our bare feet into someone else's grody shoes, we took on a bit of their story, or were free to imagine them: the Wavy Gravy concert in Sonoma, perhaps, and those suspenders walking through a crowd, crisp and bright holding up a pair of baggy pants because belts are just too mainstream, too constricting, *man*. The concert's over and the suspenders now splay in the box, untethered from history, until you pick them up, finger them, put them to work again.

BIG IDEAS

The first time I went on a writing retreat, I had no idea what I was doing. And I went for two months! I arrived at Hedgebrook on Whidbey Island, in the winter of '94, with my clunky Mac Classic in tow, a box of books, a sack full of travel journals, and lots of big ideas about writing.

I soon found out, rather painfully, that big ideas about writing often lead you nowhere. Those big ideas sit in the middle of the room, daring you to write something good. Something good and something long. They glower at you. They grumble and complain. They make you hungry just an hour after breakfast. They give you a whopping headache. They make you look at the clock and wonder if anyone would notice if you just headed home, say, seven weeks early.

The cottage had a padded window seat, a sleeping loft, a tiny woodstove, and a long desk by a window that looked into the woods. The cooks brought your lunch to you in a basket and tiptoed away. You could bicycle to Useless Bay, take long walks there accompanied by sandpipers. You could lose yourself at Useless Bay, and find yourself, and wander every which way in between. You could feel what it was like to be perfectly useless.

The pure beauty and generosity of the place made you extremely grateful and, if you're a neurotic like me, extremely guilty. What had I done to deserve such beneficence?

Though I spent much of my time at Hedgebrook fighting off my own demons, I did write my first long braided essay there: "Basha Leah," an essay that is wholly dependent on the space that grew in me during that time. It's a fragmented piece that told me, gently, that I had to give up my "big ideas" and pay attention to small details instead. It told me to sit still, to wait. It demanded that I simply be quiet.[3]

Back then you really had to dive into yourself on a writing retreat. There were very few distractions—no email, no internet, only a pay phone in the woodshed. You didn't get much mail because you wouldn't be there for long. You had yourself, and your other self, and maybe another self for company during the day (a tiresome group at best. . . .), so you looked forward with inordinate glee to conversation with other writers at the farm table at dinner. Sometimes you wandered into the kitchen early, asked if you could chop a carrot or two, just so you could feel productive at something.

If the cooks felt sympathetic that day, they'd let you. But sometimes they stuck doggedly to the rules of the place: this is a retreat from everything that is usually demanded of women. They wouldn't even let us clear our own dishes from the table, so to chop a carrot might be sacrilege. Everything was designed to keep you in the Free Box state of mind: one where the world offers itself to you freely.

So I wandered into the library, picked up a book at random: a book that began speaking to me about my hidden Jewish heritage. Then I went back to my cottage and caught a glimpse of myself in the reflection of a window as I did Tree Pose in the living room. I flipped open my notebook to a page I'd written and forgotten: about a visit to a Portuguese monastery where women pray to Mary's breast.

In the quiet I sat down to write, to weave these random things together and make use of them. To recycle. Reclaim. Such work takes time. Such work requires concentration, sniffing out the trail, crouching, examining scat for signs.

WRITING BRAIN

Now, years later, my writing brain could never crouch and wait. It's too nervous; it can barely peep out a few words. My writing brain has a kink in its neck and a sore back, it says *just let me go back to sleep*, then rouses

---

3   Being quiet is not easy when the mind is a toddler, jumping from one thing to the next, restless, eager to play.

with a groan, a recalcitrant teenager who was out past curfew last night, roaming the internet for a fix—so jumpy, as if on amphetamines, tentacles reaching outward, sticking on voices that aren't really voices, that are all an illusion, and so they exhaust this poor little brain that now just wants to sleep past noon. So you let it sleep upstairs—better a sleeping brain than a cranky brain.

The writing brain slumbers hard, drool on the pillow, but you'll shake it awake eventually and force it to come downstairs for breakfast. This brain will grumble and demand coffee and French toast. This brain will linger too long at the table, reading the paper, and when you ask it politely to get dressed, it will snap at you, *okay, okay*, and then slump into its writing clothes, heave itself into a chair, and stare blankly at the screen a while, until it whines that it needs to check Facebook and email, just in case something important has happened in the last five minutes[4]—and you'll have to be firm, set some boundaries as you have to do with all children.

You'll need to give it positive reinforcement—*see, look what a good sentence you wrote, good job!*—give it the illusion of choice—*you can either write upstairs or on the front porch, those are your choices*—and at some point you'll just have to leave the writing brain to its own devices, trust it, give it some responsibility while you watch discretely from the kitchen.

And you want to tell this brain that *freedom's just another word for nothing left to lose*, and *you don't know what you've got till it's gone*. You want to tell it to find a nice box—but not too nice—and paint it inside and out, then put inside everything that catches its eye: let the box determine how far you can go today; let the box lure you into arrangement.[5] You give your writing brain some supplies, offer what you have.

---

4 Nothing important ever happens in the last five minutes.

5 A Joseph Cornell Box resurrects what would have been lost: a key to a forgotten lock, a button, a coin, a shell, a seed pod—all these objects that litter a drawer, jumbled, dirty, but put together through intuition and a longing for harmony become something else: a story that layers time, everything existing all at once, all of it contained. I'm tempted now to jump on the internet and find some interesting factoid about Cornell to insert right here in the essay, something that will relate so coyly and perfectly to the idea of arrangement, but I just thirty seconds ago turned off the Wi-Fi in order to concentrate.

Here, you say. *Here's a free box.* But your writing brain barely looks up from its email. It sneers: *Is anything ever really free?*

THIRTEEN WAYS TO KNOW YOU NEED HELP

1. Your dog nags you. Whines urgently in her throat. *Come to bed, come to bed.*
2. You find yourself saying, aloud, "in a minute, just a minute." You keep tapping keys on your computer, your face washed in blue light.
3. One minute turns into ten turns into an hour and another. You're searching for something, but you don't know what. So many voices out there, demanding your attention, so many things that can be done. The lure of websites that promise, just one more, this next page will solve everything, but you don't even remember what you traveled here to solve.
4. By the time you do wrench yourself away, you feel wounded and confused, as if a little bit of your brain has literally torn away, shreds of it sticking to the screen.
5. You feel confused by the state of your house. Somehow, in the hours you spent online, the pile of dishes in the sink has grown, the trash has overflowed, clothes have strewn themselves on the bedroom floor. How did this happen?
6. You find yourself in front of the refrigerator, holding open the door, with no earthly idea why you're there. You go to wash the dishes, but find yourself eating a bowl of cereal instead. And now you're sitting in front of the television, watching a rerun of *The New Girl*.
7. You want to be a New Girl.
8. When you finally make it to bed, your dog looks up at you, her face a familiar mix of adoration and accusation. It's a face that says, *oh, you again, how kind of you to join us.* A face that says grumpily, *where have you been?*
9. Admit nothing. Just shove her over to her side of the bed. You've done this every night for years, but every night she acts as though

it's an affront. She sighs. She's very disappointed in you. You know things are bad when you've disappointed your dog.

10. Promise you'll do better from now on. You'll practice good "sleep hygiene" (as your doctor puts it); you'll brush your teeth, drink a cup of herbal tea, turn off all screens hours before bedtime. You'll do your yoga breathing. You'll stretch a little, put on lavender-scented moisturizer, think only good thoughts. You'll keep a tidy little dream journal by your bed, pen at the ready.

11. Instead, you fall into a fitful sleep, exhausted, as though you've been in a fight.

12. Your sleeping mind skims the surface, like a search engine, lighting here and there, dwelling in the places that get the most hits. You can't settle. You wake too early, more tired than before.

13. You look over at your dog, who sleeps with her eyes open. She sees you but doesn't see you. Her legs twitch. She chases something in her dreams.

ALONE, NOT ALONE

I'm single, and I live alone.[6] Because I live alone, when I come home the dishes that were in the sink that morning have settled there and grown crusty, the floor is still unvacuumed, and no one has cooked dinner. I look accusingly at the dog and the cat, both of whom have done literally nothing all day. They look back, all innocence, *what?*

You couldn't lift a finger? I ask. *You couldn't do a dish?*

Of course all this muttering, like the insane old lady I'm becoming, substitutes for real human interaction. And it means I go onto my email, Facebook, and other message boards to simulate this interaction all day, and long into the evening.

---

6 NPR tells me that I'm part of the fastest-growing demographic there is (it's good to feel a part of something). I listen to NPR in the morning, afternoon, and evening. There's always some voice in my ear. I half listen while doing something else. I know half-truths about a lot of things in this world. But I can never remember what I hear. I start too many conversations with phrases like: "I heard this story on NPR, I can't remember exactly what they were talking about, but it was, you know, about that *thing...*"

When you live alone, you have no other eyes (at least human eyes) to reflect back to you a picture of yourself, and that's why you start looking elsewhere: to Facebook and email and blog stats, just to feel as though you're being seen *somewhere*, somehow, but it's a funny way of doing it: so disembodied, when it's the body that craves attention. We find our homes filled with voices and conversations that evaporate when we look up. Or are those nebulous relationships just as solid now as embodied ones?

You swim each evening in this disincarnate world, occasionally coming up for air to notice the dirty dishes in the sink and the cat who needs to be fed and the dog who is sighing into her paws. You could get up and make a phone call to your mother or a friend, to hear a real voice, but no, you sink back down into the tepid waters of the internet, let yourself float there a while, your eyes flitting from one thing to the next, craving a mild commotion to greet you at the door—not this silence punctuated only by the dog's toenails on the wood floor.

BLOG

So you start a blog. A blog about the conundrum of living online and in the real world at once. A blog about being a writer, a homeowner, a teacher, a yoga student. You say your blog will be a letter to the world, becoming like a latter-day Emily Dickinson: "here is my letter to the world that never wrote to me."

But you are not Emily Dickinson. Sure, you can pull off the recluse act for a little while, but what you really want is the world to talk back to you. And talk and talk and talk.

You post something on your blog. You're a little too proud of this little post. You've found clever pictures and you've written the post in short little digestible chunks. You have a beginning, middle, and end, but it's not too long. You've read all about how people read online. You know they will skim. You have to put things in **bold.** You have lots of space. You <u>underline</u> and you ~~cross out~~.

And then you wait. You post and refresh the page. You tell everyone on Facebook: *hey, read my blog post!* You tweet it. You check for comments. You walk away for five minutes, then hurry back and check again. You look to see if anyone gave it a thumbs up.

You try to do other work, but all your work takes place on the same screen where your blog lurks. You try to swim inward but keep gasping toward the surface, looking for someone who's looking back.

MARROW

I want to write something that wonders.[7]

But I can't because all my screens are open at once. I'm all fact and surface. My eyeballs swivel in their sockets, try to look inward instead. A laser gaze, down into the esophagus, between the ribs. Beyond the bones to the marrow. Marrow: sweet, salty, dense. You have to suck it out or dig in with a small spoon. It takes some patience. It won't yield easily. You have to spend some time: focus, scrape, close your eyes to taste.

Marrow lives in the furrows, in the deepest part of you. It regenerates. You never see it until a bone breaks. But we live our lives carefully, tiptoeing along the surface, keeping what we can keep intact.

WRITING THEN, WRITING NOW

Writing used to be private. Writing used to close the door, say *excuse me*, wouldn't wash its hair for days on end. Writing put on no lipstick. Writing avoided eye contact, gazed at her toes, mumbled one-word answers when asked.

Now writing has become gregarious. Writing wants an audience. Writing wants to practice in front of the mirror.

Writing used to moon about, hugging a pillow. Writing used to lip-synch to Simon and Garfunkel, *I will lay me dooooowwwnnnn. . . .*

Now writing does karaoke. It gets up on the bar to dance.

Writing used to wait. Writing used to be patient. Writing had to go to the library, open the wooden drawers of the card catalog. Writing walked

---

7   The space for wondering has shut down, with our hardly being aware of it; as soon as someone says "I wonder. . . ." the smartphones get whipped out. The space between knowing and not-knowing has shrunk to the size of a hair.

its fingers along the yellowed edges. The library, quiet. The library like the inside of a body, where something gestates.

Now, Writing asks questions in a loud voice. Writing snaps its fingers in the library. Writing strides into the library and demands answers. The library hums. There is nothing like silence in the library. There is no body, no gestation, only spontaneous births.

TRUCE

I've been on many, many writing retreats since that first long retreat at Hedgebrook, but the nature of retreats for me has changed gradually over the years. They've grown shorter, for one thing (thank god), and I often now go on writing retreat with a friend, at a place called the Whiteley Center on San Juan Island, where we fall into an easy routine, supporting one another in our work. I'm finding that I no longer need to see writing as a purely solitary act; in fact, I can get too mired in myself.

And now it's rare to find a writing retreat where Wi-Fi is not on tap.

I resisted this for a long time, stubbornly trying to maintain inner quiet, but I always succumb. I think this sense of being constantly connected has changed what I write—I don't really know if I could write an essay like "Basha Leah" again—but new forms emerge when I do a dance with technology rather than try to wrestle it to the ground.

For example, the last time I retreated to Whiteley, I stayed for a mere five days.

And in that time, I ended up writing an essay called "36 Holes," and I wrote it almost entirely while glued to the internet. I was watching a live video feed of the rescue of the Chilean miners who had been trapped underground for months. I watched, I cried, I wrote, I watched some more. I couldn't tear myself away from the internet, so I allowed the internet to tear into me.

I thought about holes. Holes that yield treasure and those that do not. These holes accumulated as I watched the earth burp forth the missing. I kept writing them down. I rearranged them. I created a box to contain them.

And something new was forged in those five days: a peace treaty, perhaps, an inching toward a truce between outward and inward connection.

TROUBLED WATER

I'm in my bedroom listening to Simon and Garfunkel sing "Bridge Over Troubled Water." Years from this moment I won't actually be sure that it's Paul Simon or Art Garfunkel,[8] it may have been *Bread*, or Carole King, or any of those bands from the early 70s[9] who sang of longing and friendship and pain with such earnestness. But that doesn't matter, because for now I'm listening with my eyes closed, my hand in a fist over my heart, and I'm exquisitely alone.

The chenille bedspread is a prickly massage on the backs of my thighs. The air has settled into the stagnant pause that occurs after my mother has vacuumed, the whole house smelling of dust unsettled and Pledge. Now my mother might be sitting at the kitchen table with the newspaper, or outside watering the lemon trees.

Like a bridge over troubled water. . . . Somehow, though I'm just ten years old[10] I know about troubled waters, but I don't know how one

---

8 I always empathized with Art the most: he was the geeky, quiet guy, providing backup. He looked to Paul to take the lead. But I knew that, within him, he yearned for his moment in the spotlight. If I allowed myself on the internet right now, I would insert some relevant fact about the first solo album Garfunkel released—I would find its name and somehow connect that name with the project I'm undertaking now; I would try to download tracks; I would follow a trail that would probably lead to a dead end, but there might be a line or two I could glean. But I've turned off the internet. I'm here with just my geeky self, remembering an even geekier girl hugging a pillow and wailing *I will lay me dooooowwwnnnn.* . . .

9 Oh, how I long to look up the 70s! What marvelous details I'd encounter: the hair, the cars, the television shows! It's all waiting for me there: a treasure trove, a Free Box. I want to rummage. I feel it itching there in my fingertips.

10 Am I ten? If I had the internet on, I would look up the release date of *Bridge over Troubled Water*. But I have to rely on my shoddy memory instead. Perhaps I'll look it up later, if I remember. But these days, if I don't do something at the *exact* moment I think it, it never gets done. The memory cells are diuretic. They flush out input almost immediately.

becomes a bridge across them, or how to woo a Paul Simon to sing me over to the other side. I suspect there are troubled waters elsewhere in the house, turbulent rapids, though the roar is distant and muted.

When you're weary, feeling small.... Weariness should be a grown-up feeling, I know this even then, yet here weariness lives, sighing through my bones.

I want my mother, and I don't want my mother. There it is. Caught between the desire to be alone and the desire to be connected. A gap I'll inhabit the rest of my life.[11]

The smell of Pledge. The dust, a taste in my mouth. My mother obliterating all traces of dirt, scrubbing the sink clean. I hear her now, the faint sound of water running into a pot, the refrigerator door opening and closing with its soft whoosh. I can taste stuffed cabbage, the tang of sauerkraut.

Years from this moment I'll want my mother. I'll be vacuuming my own house or wiping down the dusty coffee table with Pledge, or making tomato sauce—and there she'll be, a mother at the bedroom door, listening to the faint melody of "Bridge Over Troubled Water." I'll look up from what I'm doing and say to the dog, "I've got to call my mother," and just then the phone will ring and I'll pick it up, and she'll say, "Hello, it's your mother."

I want to be a bridge over troubled water, but this bridge is built plank by plank, a suspension bridge that hangs improbably in midair. It looks like it could never hold the weight of a single person traversing side to side, not to mention two or three or hundreds of people chattering in your ear.

It's the kind of bridge that would vanish in an instant.[12] Like the movies I watch, where the heroine makes it, but the bridge disappears before the villains can traverse it. She now finds herself alone on the other side.

I'm on your siiiiiide.... And I've somehow decided—in that room, the record spinning in its wobbly way on the pink record player—that I must

---

11 And into that gap rides the internet, with its promise to be the bridge: Alone not alone. Isolatedconnected. In two places at once.

12 As a kid, we walked on such a bridge somewhere, I can't remember, and my brother, as kids do, swayed it from side to side. I laughed in my terror, trying not to gaze down at the turbulent waters below. My mother held my shoulder in a death grip.

shoulder everything alone, even in the midst of family. Even while my mother makes dinner and waits for me to open the door.

FREE BOX

I sometimes think about writing this way: as though I'm still standing on a porch decades ago, the heavy lid in my hands, rummaging and rummaging, until some unexpected thing winks at me, tells me to pick it up, examine it for what story it can tell. Or not a story, but merely what role it might play in calming down the connective tissue in my brain. Focusing it. Making everything a little clearer.

During those Orr Springs years, I wrote in a notebook until a Brother word processor arrived via UPS: a clunky white machine that allowed you to type and see four lines at a time on a tiny, dim screen before those lines transferred to the page. It seemed like a miracle, but at the same time a little odd: processing words the way we processed basil in the Cuisinart for pesto. It was slow writing, like slow food: not meant to be gobbled quickly.

On the porch at Orr Springs, there wasn't much to distract you but your own mind. Sure, you had your to-do lists, but that list included taking a long soak in the morning, followed by a sauna and a swim. You ate breakfast while reading a book, because we didn't get a daily paper. We listened to a staticky radio station that broadcast from the Bay Area. We talked and talked and stopped talking. We chopped wood. We cleaned bathrooms. We drank tea made with weeds. We turned compost over with pitchforks, the smell ripe and promising.

So you had a lot of brain space to fill with your own musings. A brain full of ideas big and small and everything in between. And that Free Box keeps standing—solid, immoveable—ready to offer what you need. I go there now, pick up the heavy lid, smell the damp wood, the musty interior. *To you the earth yields her fruit,* Kahlil whispers to me from his perch on the internet, *and you shall not want if you but know how to fill your hands.*

The Fine Art of Containment
in Creative Nonfiction

I took ikebana lessons for many years in the basement of the city library. Ikebana is the Japanese art of floral arrangement, usually characterized by elegant forms that utilize white space to allow the nature of the materials to stand out. We'd enter this dreary room, which was transformed by buckets of whatever might be in season: branches of cherry blossoms, bunches of tulips and daffodils, sprays of Scotch broom our teacher had pruned from his neighbor's yard. Our teacher, Charles, always had a particular form in mind for us to learn, and he would demonstrate how strategic trimming and setting of the materials lead to exquisite beauty.

After he demonstrated, we needed to choose from the wide variety of containers Charles had laid out for us on the table. The ikebana artist must start with the vase, as this container determines everything. Yes, the materials are important—the blooms, the branches, the greenery—but they will not find their full expression until the artist knows what shape will contain them.

The artist assesses everything about her vase—not only the shape, but the height, the color, the texture, the depth. Then she chooses her flowers and greenery, and decides what style of ikebana she's practicing. There is *Heika*, a form that requires a tall vase and mathematical precision, with each stem in perfect ratio to the others. Another form, called *Moribuna*, might be more recognizable to the Western eye; it uses shallow containers, with flowers mounding or rising ethereally from within.

Sometimes the artist can abandon the rules—try to get away from the math—yet even free-form ikebana is determined by the vase in which it is contained. At some point, the materials create their own design, demanding surrender by the artist, nudged along by a snip here and a clip there, minor adjustments of angle and perspective. And through it all, the artist has not forgotten her container: it holds every element, so the finished piece presents itself as complete.

I'm talking about ikebana (as you may have surmised) as an analogy to describe how we either consciously or intuitively create containers in our writing, a solid base from which organic beauty and meaning can emerge. Many arts have built-in forms: think of the painter's canvas, which holds the composition with the first brushstroke. Think of the sonata form in music, the fugue; think of the stage the dancer enters. All of these could be considered containers that begin shaping a work from the outset. And poets have always used solid forms—the sonnet, the villanelle, the sestina—as a way to firmly shape the materials within. Often, the more emotional or abstract the material, the more constraining the vessel can be.

In creative nonfiction writing, it can be tempting to think we don't need form; after all, isn't life itself a big enough form all on its own? Sadly, it is not. We usually need to contain our stories in smaller forms that will provide shape and movement. For the purposes of this essay, I'll focus on what I've come to call "container scenes," or through-lines, that hold the narratives within. We might also call these containers "plots" the way we would in fiction. These container scenes create both boundaries and forward movement for material that might otherwise have a hard time finding its focus. The scene also becomes the "occasion" for both writing and reading the essay. What sets us on our way? Where are we, and why?

Let's start with something simple from the past: Virginia Woolf's iconic essay "Street Haunting." You may recall that this meditative essay begins with a quotidian purpose:

> No one perhaps has ever felt passionately towards a lead pencil. But there are circumstances in which it can become supremely desirable to possess one; moments when we are set upon having an object, an excuse for walking half across London between tea and dinner.

These may, arguably, be some of the best first lines in personal essay history. With them, Woolf draws us in with a small physical item—the pencil—in a tone of wry humor, and she creates a reason for the essay that follows; a physical reason that sets us (both writer and reader) moving. She then embarks on the walk with a purpose, and somehow we become an intricate part of this quest; the ensuing essay proceeds in the first-person plural—"we." And she sets up the exact, preferred setting, alerting us to the fact that this is not a singular walk but a representative one:

> The hour should be the evening and the season winter, for in winter the champagne brightness of the air and the sociability of the streets are grateful. . . . We are no longer quite ourselves. As we step out of the house on a fine evening between four and six, we shed the self our friends know us by and become part of that vast republican army of anonymous trampers, whose society is so agreeable after the solitude of one's own room.

What follows is a meditation on the nature of that self, triggered by the sights and people she encounters on this walk. She finds herself to be permeable—not *one* self at all. Her empathy is ignited, as is her curiosity and imagination. She muses:

> Is the true self this which stands on the pavement in January, or that which bends over the balcony in June? Am I here, or am I there? Or is the true self neither this nor that, neither here nor there, but something so varied and wandering that it is only when we give the rein to its wishes and let it take its way unimpeded that we are indeed ourselves?

A heady, abstract thought that rises from the most mundane of quests: the acquisition of a pencil. After being distracted again and again on our way across London—privy to the intimate lives taking place behind lit windows—we finally return triumphant with pencil in hand:

> Here again is the usual door; here the chair turned as we left it and the china bowl and the brown ring on the carpet. And here—let us examine it tenderly, let us touch it with reverence—is the only spoil we have retrieved from all the treasures of the city, a lead pencil.

So not only has the essay taken on the container of the walk—an essay form well recognized throughout literary history (think Thoreau or Hazlitt or Alfred Kazin)—the piece meanders full circle, ending nearly *exactly* where it began: with the image of that lead pencil. But this image does not so much a repeat as transform, taking on new dimensions through the passage we've undertaken.

Turning to a more contemporary writer, Ryan Van Meter, we can see how he contains his narrative both physically and structurally in the space of a short car ride. In his essay "First" (which indeed opens as the first essay in his collection *If You Knew Then What I Know Now*), Van Meter uses present tense to create a vivid container scene in which a narrative of awakening will take place:

> Ben and I are sitting side by side in the very back of his mother's station wagon. We face glowing white headlights of cars following us, our sneakers pressed against the back hatch door. This is our joy—his and mine—to sit turned away from our moms and dads in this place that feels like a secret, as if they are not even in the car with us. They have just taken us out to dinner, and now we are driving home. Years from this evening, I won't actually be sure that this boy sitting beside me is named Ben. But that doesn't matter tonight. What I know for certain right now is that I love him, and I need to tell him this fact before we return to our separate houses, next door to each other. We are both five.

Van Meter is doing a lot of work in that first paragraph. He sets up the literal, physical container—an enclosed space (the way-back of a station wagon)—while also starting the container scene of the car ride, which includes a time element that adds urgency. Through strategic use of the future tense, he also drops in the presence of the older narrator looking back and recreating this memory, as well as seeding the prevalent theme that will resonate through the essay: secrets.

The entire essay takes place within the nested containers of that station wagon and the five-minute car ride home. The author takes his time fully developing the setting and the motion, using sensory details such as Ben's "T-ball bat rolling around and clunking" and Ben's "perpetually undone shoelaces." He gives us the sound of the adults murmuring, the baseball game on the radio. Ben and Ryan are holding hands and "there is something sticky on his fingers, probably the strawberry syrup from the ice cream sundaes we ate for dessert." He wants to see their hands but "they are only visible every block or so when the car passes beneath a streetlight, and then only for a flash."

Branching off from this present-tense scene, Van Meter uses past tense to describe his summer afternoons at home with his mother watching soap operas and learning about the melodramatic, all-consuming nature of love. This context allows us to understand more fully what is happening in the container scene: the young Ryan is a boy in love with another boy. He is holding hands with him, and he gets up the courage to finally say, in the sanctum of that station wagon, what he's been yearning for all along. The scene slows down and becomes suspended there, just as the car slows to a stop at a red light.

"I love you," I say. We are idling, waiting for a red light to be green; a shining car has stopped right behind us, so Ben's face is pale and brilliant.

"I love you too," he says.

The car becomes quiet as the voice of the baseball game shrinks smaller and smaller.

"Will you marry me?" I ask him. His hand is still in mine; on the soap opera you're supposed to have a ring, but I don't have one.

This interchange attracts the attention of the adults, who begin to intrude on the "secret" space the two boys have inhabited, and this space seems to now become even *more* confining: a trap rather than a pleasure. Ryan's mother turns and asks him to repeat himself. Again, this moment, which would pass in a flash in "real life," is suspended within the motion of the car ride. The young Ryan says, "I brace myself against the raised carpeted hump of the wheel well as Ben's father turns left onto the street before the turn onto my street." The clock is ticking. And then this:

> I am still facing my mother, who is still facing me, and for one last second, we look at each other without anything wrong between us.

The entire essay has led to this moment, this turning point. We pause, waiting for what will happen next, what the reader knows will happen next, what the boy narrator intuits will happen next. She tells him that "boys don't marry other boys." Ben pulls away from him: "To be back here in the private tail of the car suddenly feels wrong, and Ben and I each scoot off to our separate sides."

The essay ends, as it must, with the end of the car ride. We have gone from point A to point B, both literally and metaphorically:

> The car starts to dip as we head down the hill of our street; our house is at the bottom. No one speaks for the rest of the ride. We all just sit and wait and watch our own views of the road — the parents see what is ahead of us, while the only thing I can look at is what we have just left behind.

So, this essay fully utilizes both containers: a small place (the way-back of the station wagon) and a short amount of time (the car ride). Often one of the most difficult skills in personal nonfiction writing is knowing where and when to suspend important moments so we can fully inhabit them. By containing his narrative into a constricted space, Van Meter paradoxically has *more* room to expand a singular moment in time, to hone in on a turning point that in reality may have passed too quickly to even register, but in writing can be shaped to provide a new understanding for both writer and reader.

Sometimes, the container scene might be enacted more subtly, becoming clear only as the essay progresses. Brent Staples's short essay "The Coroner's Photographs" begins with the narrator viewing photographs of his younger brother in the morgue:

> My brother's body lies dead and naked on a stainless steel slab. . . . His head is squarish and overlarge. (This, when he was a toddler, made him seem top-heavy and unsteady on his feet.). . . . His eyes (closed here) were big and dark and glittery; they drew you into his sadness when he cried.

Staples uses the coroner's report to detail not only his brother's death, but also his brother's life. The photographs allow the narrator and the reader to examine every detail of the brother's body, and from these details elicit the particularities of this young man's trajectory that ended here, in the morgue. He tells us that the report begins with a "terse narrative summary" and then goes on to inventory the parts of his brother's body: heart, lung, liver, spleen, brain, etc. Staples uses the nomenclature and objective tone of the report as foil to a larger emotional undercurrent—both familial and societal. Staples wants to rescue his brother from the abyss of an "ordinary death," allow him to be more than mere statistic, more than another drug dealer's violent demise:

> The lips are ajar as always, but the picture is taken from such an angle that it misses a crucial detail: the left front tooth tucked partly beyond the right one. I need this detail to see my brother full. I paint it in from memory.

While the ostensible container for this essay might be the coroner's report itself (a scientific tool of detachment), Staples also creates a contained structure in the shape of an ouroboros—the ancient symbol of a snake swallowing its own tail. In the closing paragraph of the essay, we see Staples at the moment he receives the report, pulling out the photographs:

I asked to see the files. A secretary brought a manila pouch and handed it to the Commonwealth Attorney, who handed it to me and excused himself from the room. The pouch contained a summary of the trial, the medical examiner's report, and a separate inner pouch wrapped in twine and shaped like photographs. I opened the pouch; there was Blake dead on the slab, photographed from several angles. The floor gave way, and I fell down for miles.

In these lines, we discover that the entire essay has actually been taking place in one contained scene: those few moments in the attorney's office, when Staples encounters the photographs for the first time. This scene has been shaping the essay from the outset, though we entered it *in medias res*.

The final images lead the reader right back to the beginning of the essay, which as you may recall, starts with the line, "My brother's body lies dead and naked on a stainless steel slab." The ouroboros symbolizes the cycle of life—the way we can often find neither beginning nor end, but instead must surrender to the momentum of rotation. In this essay, Staples conveys an experience that cannot be satisfactorily concluded; instead, the images will stay with him forever, startling him with new emotion, new memories, new meanings. He (and the reader) will now always be witnesses, and so the essay loops back around and begins again.

While a short essay might lend itself to being restricted inside small vessels, container scenes can also be particularly useful when holding together a longer essay that moves through time and space. In some instances, the container scene can be broken into simple bookends. For example, in his essay "Burl's," from his memoir *Truth Serum*, Bernard Cooper uses the act of going out to fetch a newspaper from the vending machine outside a diner as a "serving platter," if you will, for an extended meditation on gender and sexual identity. The essay begins with a vivid, representative description of Burl's, the diner where the young Cooper and his parents often ate in the summertime. The narrative then switches from a representative to a specific scene, signaled by the phrase

"One evening": "One evening, annoyed with my restlessness, my father gave me a dime and asked me to buy him a *Herald Examiner* from the vending machine in front of the restaurant." Cooper does so, changing locales from interior to exterior:

> Shouldering open the heavy glass door, I was seared by a sudden gust of heat. Traffic roared past me and stirred the air. Walking toward the newspaper machine, I held the dime so tightly, it seemed to melt in my palm. Duty made me feel large and important. I inserted the dime and opened the box, yanking a *Herald* from the spring contraption that held it tight as a mousetrap. When I turned around, paper in hand, I saw two women walking toward me.

These two women—who, as they come closer, reveal themselves as having the gender markers of men—will be the trigger for Cooper's memories of his own confusion about gender roles and sexuality. With his characteristic profusion of sensory detail, Cooper takes his time, extending the active description of the two women passing him on the sidewalk for another two pages. Such lines as "Dangling earrings flashed in the sun, brilliant as prisms" show the narrator's keen, observant eye as he zeros in on various elements until he sees a "rift" that reveals the characters' maleness: "I saw that her jaw was heavily powdered, a half-successful attempt to disguise the telltale shadow of a beard." As Van Meter does with his way-back of the station wagon, so does Cooper with his sidewalk encounter: he suspends the moment so that we experience it seemingly in real time, signaling the thematic significance of this encounter: "Any woman might be a man; the fact of it clanged through the chambers of my brain."

After a section break, the essay travels back in time to enact three key scenes tied to this theme: an incident in his parents' closet when he is caught trying on his mother's clothes; an attempt by his parents to make Cooper more "boy-like" by enrolling him in a gymnastics class at the Athletic Club; and an encounter with a male stranger who ogles the young Cooper at a bus stop. After moving through these events, we return, after another section break, to the original errand, which we've almost forgotten:

I handed my father the *Herald*. He opened the paper and disappeared behind it. My mother stirred her coffee and sighed. . . . For a moment, I considered asking them about what had happened on the street, but they would have reacted with censure and alarm, and I sensed there was more to the story than they'd ever be willing to tell me. Men in dresses were only the tip of the iceberg. . . . It would be years before I heard the word *transvestite*, so I struggled to find a word for what I'd seen. . . . *Burl's* would have been perfect, like *boys* and *girls* spliced together, but I can't claim to have thought of this back then.

Within the simplest of plot lines—go out to get the paper; get the paper; return with the paper—Cooper is able to organize significant scenes to create a cohesive essay. And in these last few moments, the adult narrator makes an appearance: the shaping consciousness who sees in retrospect how the diner itself (this large, physical container) announces the predominant theme in its very name.

A strategic container scene can be particularly useful when piecing together a segmented or braided essay; the container scene acts as a through-line on which the writer can attach both past-tense and future-tense scenes. In another essay, "Imitation of Life," Cooper uses a plot line involving his mother's Kenmore chest freezer as an anchor: we see his mother longing for a freezer, then her acquiring that freezer, filling it with food, and gradually abandoning the freezer once her health issues make it impossible to maintain. Interspersed within this simple plot are scenes that elucidate Cooper's relationship with his mother, and his hunger to both fit in and stand apart. The essay travels widely through time and space, but returns again and again to that freezer: a literal container of abundance, nurturance, and desire.

For my final example, I want to discuss what happens when the material seems so charged that it wants to blow apart containers altogether, smashing them to smithereens.

Karen Green's lyric memoir *Bough Down* is an account of the aftermath of her husband's suicide (her husband happened to be David Foster Wallace, but she never mentions him by name). Green is a poet, and her poet's training serves her well here as we experience—through imagery and fragmentation—the dislocation of grief.

The book is laid out with an abundance of white space and gaps, the text often floating in space. But even with fragmentation as her intentional methodology, the story's need to be contained, to start *somewhere*, is evident:

> June, Black
>> Does it begin like this . . . ?
>> The mouth of the Volvo opens to reveal something coiled: cotton paisley affixed to the garden hose with electrical tape. Your simulated overnight bag reeks of American Spirits, a few fuzzy pills caught in the seams. On the back burner, a mercury-filled tooth crumbles. Garden ants draw vibrating, teeming strips up and down the artichoke stalks. The support guys are in the thick of the starless forest; they catch and release. They call the crows blackbirds. The kind black dog sighs on my shin, sighs on my thigh, relieved and relieved, forever home. Sharpie, ink, humor, hole. Fat widows spin chaos on the patio, their thoracic hourglasses graphic red flags. Here is fruit for the crow, but that will come later.

The text embarks with a question of beginnings, in a text where beginning and ending become illusory. Actually, the narrative begins even *before* that question, with two markers—one in time ("June"), a month that often evokes new beginnings, the gladness of summer; the other a color ("Black") that evokes mourning and grief—and thus the tension between opposites is seeded as a theme from the very first words. In this opening salvo we also see right away that Green will be addressing her late husband, her grief taking the form of questions and confusion.

The rest of the paragraph consists of disjointed images, beginning with "the mouth of the Volvo opens to reveal something coiled"—an image that elicits something dangerous, something that can't be apprehended at first glance, and ending with fruit for the crows, an image that evokes rot and decay. The color black recurs directly and indirectly—blackbirds and black dogs; "Sharpies, ink, humor, hole": all of which can be modified by the adjective "black." Here we experience a narrator struggling to make sense of the senseless by naming what she can name. She mentions pills in passing; these pills will reappear throughout the book. This associative style reflects the emotional tenor of the work that will come: life has fractured, and the representation of that life must explode in response.

The book proceeds in fits and starts as Green tries to return to "normal" life. But not even language can suffice; she creates visual collages and inserts them throughout the book, the text literally cut into fragments, with words sputtered and obscured: "Why did you" and "the poor dogs" and "the coroner said not fresh."

Yet, paradoxically perhaps, though the narrative *appears* formless and untethered, the restrictions of the page, the paragraph, and the collage canvas create very small containers that hold, tightly, the material within. The tension between the smallness of the containers and the enormity of what they try to contain is a large part of what makes this text so powerful.

For example—this small fragment, which appears on its own page, surrounded by white space—evokes an entire scene to which we have no real access:

> I worry I broke your kneecaps when I cut you down. I keep hearing that sound. We fly from the world, right, like shrapnel angels, but why is everything so laden around here?
>
> Your legs were elegant, and your crossed them elegantly, not like a boy pretending his jewels were too big.

The actual scene, the full story, lies outside the restricted lines of the paragraphs, simmers inside the white space. These snippets focus on small concrete details rather than the abstractions of emotion, the way one might go over and over certain details in our minds after a trauma. Green is cordoning off her memory, containing it as one might a wild animal, so that it doesn't destroy her (though it kind of destroys us).

I'll leave off with one more thought from visual artist George Bellows: "Art strives for form and hopes for beauty." Rather than aiming for beauty, we must first find the forms that enable beauty and meaning to emerge from amorphous reality.

Think of the word "reform": how the word, itself, connotes improving, mending, or restoration—we send unruly children to reform school, so they might learn how best to contain themselves. When we've strayed off the best path, we promise to "reform," to shape up. And the same is true with our writing: we must re-form our material—shape it again and again, until we've found a synergy of container and content.

Think about the times you've brought home flowers or picked them from your yard; you bring them inside, find the vase, assess how best to show them off. But what happens when you rummage through the cupboards and find no container? You would still have your beautiful materials, but it might be more difficult to find their common purpose. You might just dump them in a jar, allow them to fall where they may, but even that gesture is an act of containment. We rarely leave the blooms simply scattered on a countertop; that would be considered a mess, something to be disregarded or thrown away. And the flowers wouldn't last as long, exposed as they are to the elements—stems cut, grasping for something to sustain them.

The Shared Space Between Reader and Writer:

A Case Study

I often teach classes specifically on the form of the "hermit crab" essay. Hermit crab essays adopt already existing forms as the container for the writing at hand, such as the essay in the form of a "to-do" list, or a field guide, or a recipe. Hermit crabs are creatures born without their own shells to protect them; they need to find empty shells to inhabit (or sometimes not so empty; in the years since I coined the term "hermit crab" as my metaphor, I've learned that they can be quite vicious, evicting the shell's rightful inhabitant by force).

When I teach the Hermit Crab class, we begin by brainstorming the many different forms that exist for us to plunder for our own purposes. Once we have such a list scribbled on the board, I ask the students to choose one form at random and see what kind of content that form suggests. This is the essential move: allowing form to dictate content. By doing so, we get out of our own way; we bypass what our intellectual minds have already determined as "our story" and instead become open and available to unexpected images, themes, and memories. Also, following the dictates of form gives us creative nonfiction writers a chance to practice using our imaginations, filling in details, and *playing* with the content to see what kind of effects we can create.

I've taught the Hermit Crab class many, many times over the years, in many different venues. So, often it's tempting for me to sit out the exercise; after all, what else could I *possibly* learn? But after just a minute, it becomes too boring to watch other people write, so I dive in myself, with no expectation that I'll write anything "good." In one class, I glanced at the board we had filled with dozens of forms. And my eye landed on "rejection notes." So that is where I began:

April 12, 1970

Dear Young Artist:

Thank you for your attempt to draw a tree. We appreciate your efforts, especially the way you sat patiently on the sidewalk, gazing at that tree for an hour before setting pen to paper, the many quick strokes of charcoal executed with enthusiasm. But your drawing looks nothing like a tree. In fact, the smudges look like nothing at all, and your own pleasure and pride in said drawing are not enough to redeem it. We are pleased to offer you remedial training in the arts, but we cannot accept your "drawing" for display.

> With regret and best wishes,
> The Art Class
> Andasol Avenue Elementary School

Well, once one gets on the subject of rejection, you can imagine how the material simply *flows* through one's fingertips. And I'm not really thinking about the content at all; I'm engaged in honing the voice of the rejection note, creating a persona on the page that can "speak back" to me, in a humorous way, all that had gone unspoken in real life. I'm having an immensely good time.

Here's one that comes early on in the essay:

October 13, 1975

Dear 10th Grader:

Thank you for your application to be a girlfriend to one of the star players on the championship basketball team. As you can imagine, we have received hundreds of similar requests and so cannot possibly respond personally to every one. We regret to inform you that you have not been chosen for one of the coveted positions, but we do invite you to continue hanging around the lockers, acting as if you belong there. This selfless act serves the team members as they practice the art of ignoring lovesick girls.

> Sincerely,
> The Granada Hills Highlanders

P.S.: Though your brother is one of the star players, we could not take this familial relationship into account. Sorry to say no! Please do try out for one of the rebound girlfriend positions in the future.

So I'm going along chronologically, calling up (and enhancing, exaggerating, manipulating) all the slights and hurts of an ordinary life. I'm having a marvelous time, because this voice is so detached it can say whatever it wants. I'm submitting to the voice of the essay, allowing the form to lead me where it will go.

And as I follow that voice, the notes begin to demand more room, wanting to break free of the concise form and allow for a more in-depth story. Now that I've established the voice of the form, I can expand on that voice to create more variety and narrative. I can also broaden the concept of the rejection note to create sections that work for the subject matter. For example:

December 10, 1978

Dear College Dropout:

Thank you for the short time you spent with us. We understand that you have decided to terminate your stay, a decision that seems completely reasonable given the circumstances. After all, who knew that the semester you decided to come to UC Berkeley would be so tumultuous: that unsavory business with Jim Jones and his Bay Area followers, the mass suicide, an event that left us all reeling. After all, who among us has not mistakenly followed the wrong person, come close to swallowing poison?

And then Harvey Milk was shot. A blast reverberating across the bay. It truly did feel like the world was falling apart, we know that. We understand how you took refuge in the music of the Grateful Dead, dancing until you felt yourself leave your body behind, caught up in their brand of enlightenment. But you understand that's only an illusion, right?

And given that you were a drama major, struggling on a campus well known for histrionics and unrest: well, it's only understandable that you'd need some time to "find yourself." You're really too young to be in such a city on your own. When you had your exit interview with the dean of students, you were completely inarticulate about your reasons for leaving, perhaps because you really have no idea. You know there is a boy you might love, living in Santa Cruz. You fed him peanuts at a Dead show. You imagine playing house with him, growing up there in the shadows of large trees.

But of course you couldn't say that to the dean, as he swiveled in his chair, so official in his gray suit. He clasped his hands on the oak desk and waited for you to explain yourself. His office looked out on the quad where you'd heard the Talking Heads playing just a week earlier. And just beyond that, the dorm where the gentleman you know as "Pink Cloud" provided you with LSD so you would experience more fully the secrets the Dead whispered in your ear. You told the dean none of this, simply shrugged your shoulders and began to cry. At which point the dean cleared his throat and wished you luck.

We regret to inform you that it will take quite a while before you grow up, and it will take some cataclysmic events of your own before you really begin to find the role that suits you. In any case, we wish you the best in all your future educational endeavors.

Sincerely,
UC Berkeley Registrar

And then, as the years go by, I find that the essay is leading me somewhere I didn't expect. I actually pause and say to the essay, "We're really going there?" and the essay says, *of course we are!* So, I find myself here:

October 26, 1979

Dear Potential Mom,

Thank you for providing a host home for us for the few weeks we stayed in residence. It was lovely but, in the end, didn't quite work for us. While we tried to be unobtrusive in our exit, the narrowness of your fallopian tubes required some damage. Sorry about that. You were too young to have children anyway, you know that, right? And you know it wasn't your fault, not really . . . still, we enjoyed our brief stay in your body and wish you the best of luck in conceiving children in the future.

> With gratitude,
> *Ira and Isabelle*

So, as you can tell, the essay takes a turn there, or maybe "turn" is not the right word, but it slows down and peers below the surface. It tells me this is where we were going all along. I've written about this material so many times in the past, that I didn't feel I would ever return to it. But the essay demanded it, and who am I to question the ferocity of an essay in progress?

And this time I feel a kind of transformation happening, a new perspective, a moment of forgiveness. It's odd to feel this in one's writing, to feel so concretely that the essay is indeed in charge: speaking to you, telling you things you didn't already know. And this happened solely because of the form. The form of the rejection note—though it began as a technical exercise—created an entirely new universe in which your personal narrative does not really belong to you. And because it doesn't belong to you, it can create meanings—perhaps better meanings—than any you might have thought up on your own.

The essay, now titled "We Regret to Inform You" (what else *could* it be?), moves, as it must, as life does, quickly through this time period. It has created its own momentum and can't stop now! The essay has also now provided me with a theme that can echo through the rest of the sections. For example:

June 30, 1999

Dear Applicant:

Thank you for your query about assuming the role of stepmother to two young girls. While we found much to admire in your résumé, we regret to inform you that we have decided not to fund the position this year. You did ask for feedback on your application, so we have the following to suggest:

1. You do not yet understand the delicate emotional dynamic that rules a divorced father's relationship with his children. The children will always, *always*, come first, trumping any needs you yourself may have at the time. You will understand this in a few years, but for now you still require some apprenticeship training.
2. Though you have sacrificed time and energy to support this family, it's become clear that your desire to stepmother stems from some deep-seated wound in yourself, a wound you are trying to heal by using these children. Children are intuitive, though they may not understand what they intuit. They have enough to deal with—an absent mother, a frazzled father—they don't need your traumas entering the mix.
3. Seeing the movie *Stepmom* is not an actual tutorial on step-parenting.
4. On Mother's Day, you should not expect flowers, gifts, or a thank you. You are not their mother.
5. You are still a little delusional about the true potential here for a long-term relationship. The father is not yet ready to commit so soon after the rather messy divorce. (This should have been obvious to you when he refused to hold your hand, citing that it made him "claustrophobic." Can you not take a hint?)

As we said, funding is the main criteria that led to our rejection of your offer. We hope this feedback is helpful, and we wish you the best in your future parenting endeavors.
        XXX OOO

Through several revisions of the draft—which included nearly twice as many letters as represented in the final version (as I said, once you get on the subject of rejection, you can really go on and on and on)—I honed the themes I saw rising in the essay through, or perhaps in spite of, the harsh voice of the rejection note. There was the ostensible theme of children or lack thereof, but more insistently there was the theme of how we find the roles we are suited to play in our lives. So I kept the letters that had echoes of that theme and deleted the rest. I highlighted the theme through key words and phrases to create a fragmented piece that felt coherent and satisfying.

Throughout the process—both drafting and revising—I did not feel the emotional weight of *any* of the material. In fact, I was laughing most of the time, inordinately pleased with my cleverness. Humor naturally arises when we couple a detached voice with intimate stories, and since audiences are also usually laughing throughout the essay, the weight of that turn in the middle almost has *more* impact than if I had started with this material as the destination. And we get through it quickly. It's one moment in a series of moments that accumulate to a greater end.

So, the essay gets published in *The Sun*, and I receive lots of responses, more than I've ever received for any essay in my life. I've written about a lot of personal material, but this one seems to have struck a deeper chord. And I think people are touched by "We Regret to Inform You" not because of the revelation of my personal "rejections," but because I've used a form that invites readers into both my experience and their own. By being ensconced in a more "objective" form, the essay provides what I'll call a "shared space" between reader and writer. We often wonder how to make our personal stories universal; well, perhaps it's not a question of "making" our stories do anything. Maybe, instead, we simply need to provide common ground in the form of an object we use together. We sit down at the same table and the stories pass between us.

SECTION THREE

In Memoriam

I want to tell you about a class I took over thirty years ago. I want you to see the class gathering: about twenty women, finding their seats, and at the front of the room, the teacher, Pesha Gertler, resplendent in her layers of flowing clothes, writing a quote on the board. That board will hold many such quotes in the years to come, as I take this class over and over at a local community college: Self-Discovery for Women through Creative Writing. College didn't quite work out for me, so here I am, in my late twenties, searching for something, not sure what. The tables have been arranged in a large rectangle, all of us finding our seats, facing one another, ready for anything.

Over the years, I must have taken the course in many different seasons, but I always remember it as winter, driving out to North Seattle Community College on the dark and damp streets after a day working in an office for an Italian espresso company. I answered phones and typed up invoices on an old electric Remington, flirted with the salesmen and the vendors, made coffee for prospective customers. It wasn't a demanding job, and in the intervals between work I typed out stories of my own on that rackety typewriter, using Wite-Out to correct my many mistakes.

I came home to an old house I shared with three strangers, and my room populated with only a twin bed and a writing desk that faced a window looking out on Green Lake. I think about that girl now, a young woman who worked for four years at a hippy resort in California, then drifted her way to Seattle. A young woman who backpacks by herself nearly every weekend in the summer. A young woman who somehow keeps finding herself drawn back to writing but not really knowing how.

So she drives every week to North Seattle to enter this classroom, which is transformed by Pesha's intention and energy, her flowing clothes, and her soft-spoken voice, slightly accented like the voices of my grandmothers, and when all of us arrive we know we're entering what can only be described as sacred space, which means we leave the work-aday world behind us. We read a poem together, then write, just write, for an hour in silence, following whatever prompt Pesha had given us for the night. I wish I could remember some of them now, but it wasn't the trigger that was important, but where we went with it, all of us shedding our skins, writing deep, then sharing.

I remember sharing something I wrote about my grandmother; I hear myself reading a line I don't remember writing, though it was just a moment ago: "... as if her hands held a warding touch and would keep me safe forever." The words ring in the silence, and some of us start to cry. Crying not for the loss of my grandmother, but because I've stumbled onto something here, what we might call my authentic voice. A voice that has burrowed out of the litter and understands the power of rhythm and cadence and image.

Sometimes it was hard. Sometimes it was so uncomfortable that one evening, when my anxiety emerged full force, I actually crawled under the table to get away and out the door; Pesha looked at me bemused above her reading spectacles, just nodding, knowing we all had to do what we had to do. But most often I was able to stay in that room, to keep the pen moving for an hour.

It was the first time I felt the solid connection between pen and paper, hand and mind. How this process of simply writing—without judgment and in the company of others—opens some hidden chamber that holds all your forgotten memories, a place undamaged by time. A place like a cave in an Indiana Jones movie, glistening with treasure. A place that takes some ingenuity and perseverance to find: flying past maraud-ers determined to foil you, swinging from vines, jumping into miners' ore carts and careening down the tracks: this is what Pesha taught us, silently, as she did her own writing with us, glasses at the end of her nose, hair big and curly around her face. She taught us the pathways to take that would lead us into these hallowed spaces and back out again.

I've learned, since then, that nothing else really matters—not a skill with syntax or imagery, not an expansive vocabulary—if you haven't found a way, and continue to find your way, to the source, if you haven't learned to hear the sound of your own voice calling out to you from underground. And thirty years later, I find myself doing the same kind of work with my women writer friends, always returning to this elemental practice.

A couple of weeks ago, Pesha died, and the news brought me back to those days when a young woman didn't know what answers she wanted to find, only that she was one big question mark walking through the world, a question sitting at her desk, gazing out the window, wondering where she must go next.

On the Power of Your Word

I recently had a marvelous winter break, mainly because I did some writing. And the only way I did my writing was by making a contract with my writing buddy, Lee. We agreed to each write one short piece a day and send them to each other. They didn't have to be good pieces; we just had to write them.

When I returned to teaching, I started out by asking my students to tell us something fun they did over winter break. We heard stories of cross-country train excursions, indoor sky-diving, and a trip to India to help with waste-water management projects. We heard about movies and meals and time with family. Finally one of my students asked what fun thing I had done. What came out of my mouth: "I wrote ten new pieces."

I used to think I could write all by my lonesome. I used to drag myself to the writing desk and dutifully plug away until something not-so-awful emerged out of the mess. And I never called it "fun"; I called it "work." And I often said the phrase: "I'm trying to write," which is worlds away from actually writing.

When I enlist allies—in the form of contracts or writing groups—the "trying" part disappears. I no longer have to "try" to write; I simply write, because I've given my word. When you "give your word" you are essentially honoring the most authentic part of your artistic self. Your word, as they used to say, is your bond.

Some days during this contract period were easy; new pieces seemed to simply appear with little effort. Other days it might take me until late at night to come up with something; it didn't matter, though, because I was writing. And Lee was writing. Our pieces crossed in midair. We met a few times to discuss what we wrote, having lunch in our favorite café downtown. This was our reward, but the compensation of the contract was truly the writing itself.

The meaning of the word "contract" comes from the old French "to make narrow, to draw together." By establishing a contract with a writing friend, you narrow down the possibilities for your time. You draw together your intentions and multiply them. You give your word to another, and you receive your words right back.

On Friendship, Assignments, Detail, and Trust

FRIENDSHIP

It's midautumn, and I go to a bookstore café to meet with two women I don't know very well yet. We met through a service-learning program at the university, and discovered we all want more writing time, more excuses for writing. So Kim, Marion, and I gather in this café—where the service is surly and spotty—at the table next to the poetry bookshelf. This lone bookshelf is hidden away here on the top floor, almost as an afterthought, poetry relegated to a corner where it takes some effort to find it.

We're not sure how to begin. We sip our lattes, gossip about school. My eyes wander toward the poetry bookshelf, and my hand reaches out to grab a book, *Late Wife*, by Claudia Emerson. I've heard about this book, I say. Do you want to read it together?

ASSIGNMENT

So we do. And we come back together the following week, excited by her "Divorce Epistles," by the way Emerson is able to return to the past, to pain, to loss, through directly addressing the ex-husband. We all have something in our past to address, some complexity that hasn't been easily resolved, perhaps never will be. So we give each other an assignment. Write an apology, we say, to someone in your past. An "apology epistle." I'm not sure why we come up with apology. It's just the first thing to come to mind.

DETAIL

I sit down at home and write the first words, *I'm sorry* . . . And immediately the image of that piece of wood in the road comes into my mind. It doesn't arrive with a blare and a bang; it just emerges there in my brain, crystal clear, as if it had been waiting all this time for me to blink it into focus. *I'm sorry about that time I ran over a piece of wood in the road.* I haven't been thinking about my ex-boyfriend, a man I knew almost forty years ago. I had been a young woman, very young, still a child. And so, with the image of this small piece of wood, the entire relationship comes back full force, everything that had transpired between us distilled into the essence of that road trip across the desert:

> I'm sorry about that time I ran over a piece of wood in the road. A pound of marijuana in the trunk and a faulty brake light—any minute the cops might have pulled us over, so you were edgy already, and then I ran over that piece of stray lumber without even slowing down. *Thunk, thunk,* and then the wood spun behind us on the road. Your dark face dimmed even darker, and you didn't yell at first, only turned to look out the window, and I made the second mistake: *What's wrong?* That's when you exploded. *You're so careless, you don't even think, what if there had been a nail in that thing,* you yelled, your face so twisted now, and ugly. *And I'm always the one that cleans it up whenever something breaks.*

The first words, *I'm sorry* . . . lead me along and become the mantra for the rest of the piece. I was always apologizing back then, for what I'm not sure. What am I sorry about? Flashes of images come to mind, the way that young girl cowered in the trailer, sorry for so many things. I let them come, I don't censor them, because by now the essay has taken on a life of its own. The second paragraph emerges as one long line, because I can't risk stopping: I have to keep going to see where we'll end up:

> *I'm sorry,* I said, and I said it again, and we continued on our way through the desert, in the dark of night, with the contraband you had put in our trunk, with the brake light you hadn't fixed blinking on and off, me driving because you were too drunk, or too tired, or too depressed, and we traveled for miles into our future, where eventually I would apologize for the eggs being overcooked, and for the price of light bulbs, and for the way the sun blared through our dirty windows and made everything too bright, and I would apologize when I had the music on and when I had it off, I'd say sorry for being in the bathroom, and sorry for crying, and sorry for laughing, I would apologize, finally, for simply being alive, and even now I'm sorry I didn't swerve, I didn't get out of the way.

TRUST

I bring the piece, three copies, to our meeting the following week. We're all a little nervous, so we spend most of our time gossiping before turning to the pages in our hands. I read "Swerve" aloud, and as I'm reading I see what I've really written. I didn't know it until I shared it with them; I had just been following that piece of wood. But now I see that while I truly was sorry about running over it, I was really sorry for subjecting my young self to such a harsh experience.

I could never have written the essay deliberately, trying to work with all those complex emotions head-on. I simply had to trust in that piece of wood.

I had to let my intuition guide me to that dangerous place, and that last line needed to hold the force of what I'd learned in the thirty years between the event itself and the representation of that event. I was sorry I hadn't swerved to avoid a piece of wood, yes, but I was even sorrier I hadn't swerved to avoid the pain that would come to define those years of my life. The last sentence propels the speaker (and the reader) through the painful memory of the past into the present moment of forgiveness for the past.

The brief form made this little essay possible. I had been trying to write a memoir of this time, failing miserably because the weight of the emotion was too fraught and could easily veer into a sad form of therapy. Because this essay is so short, I needed to take only a slice of that time, and from this one cross-section—*I'm sorry about that time I ran over a piece of wood in the road*—I unraveled the rest.

The last line "rhymes" with the first line, echoing the apology, and yet shows a vast transformation in the narrator's perspective. Though only 264 words from the first line, we've come a long way in time and a long way in the stance of the narrator—from a young woman who is cowed to a more mature narrator who can stand up and see more clearly the forces at work in this relationship. For a short-short piece to work, the opening and ending lines must have this kind of relationship, and bring us further than we ever imagined a few lines could travel.

Cables, Chains, and Lariats:

Form as Process

It's Monday morning, and I'm where I usually am on Monday mornings: writing with my practice group in my friend Nancy Canyon's art studio. We've been meeting together for years, sometimes in a café, but lately settled into the studio where we're surrounded by Nancy's paintings: lush colors that form images of watery reflections.

We settle in quickly, using a formal writing practice technique Nancy has taught us: we each write random words or lines on scraps of paper—sometimes grabbing whatever book or brochure is handy for inspiration—and toss these in a porcelain dish, to be chosen at random at the beginning of each writing segment. The first part is five minutes, writing very short sentences. The second is ten minutes, chaining sentences, where the end word of a sentence becomes the beginning word of the next. The third is one long sentence for twenty minutes. Between the segments, we read aloud what we wrote, with no response from the listeners. At the end of the writing practice, we "speak back" to each other the images or phrases that resonated with us.

It's a simple but powerful practice. And while not everything I write will make it into finished work, it's the practice itself that becomes essential, keeping the writing mind tuned and ready. Since these women and I have written together for so long, we're able to quickly enter a deep space where we excavate memories, scenes, and images that would not have come forward on their own. The formal constraints—and the random start lines—demand that we let go of preconceived stories and follow the rhythm and waves of language wherever they might take us.

Today, as on many days, I find myself writing about the few months I spent in the Arizona desert as a young woman with a man who was bad for me. I've tried to write about this time before, with no success. But in the confines of this room—surrounded by art, by other women writing, and subservient to the assignments—fragments of this era emerge quickly on the page, no matter what start line triggers them. I'm writing fast: no time to censor or pretty up; no time to hesitate. And different voices will speak, depending on the form.

The short sentences sound like urgent telegraphs: cables from the past that necessarily must give only the important bits of information. It's a solemn voice, with no patience for hedging or clearing the throat, but a compassionate one as well, striving to deliver the news gently.

The chaining sentences coil together, forming a rhythm that captures the narrator in their own momentum. The pattern demands that she keep going forward, each sentence leading inevitably to the next, just as this girl's life back then seemed inevitable, carried forward by a force she couldn't control. Sometimes, these chains seem heavy and metallic, jailing the narrator in the story with no way out; but sometimes they remind me of daisy chains, or the small loops of colored paper we made as children, chained together to form a garland. Something that is light and transient.

The long sentence is the most demanding and the most urgent. We have to breathe as we write, and use lots of conjunctions, and keep up our stamina; we can't stop even when we've reached a dead end; we have to keep moving, keep searching, ride the galloping horse of the sentence with a lariat in hand, seeking out the image that will get us out of here in one piece.

Later, at home by myself, I'll be able to turn to the notebooks and see what I've written. I always have someplace to start, my handwriting like tracks I follow in the sand. I have to make some decisions about what gets typed up and what does not. I'll need to decide whether I can keep the fragments in the form that triggered them, or revise so the prose makes more narrative or aesthetic sense. But still, the forms will continue to infuse the pieces with a particular tone or rhythm that contributes to the essay's meaning.

Since we are writing in short bursts, this practice lends itself to the short-short form, relying on language, rhythm, and image, much as poetry does. Sometimes I wonder if these fragments can ever add up to anything, but once I've assembled dozens of them together, I can see the patterns emerge. I arrange and rearrange, notice repeating imagery, combine and cut apart. The story that develops is one that follows a logic beyond the intellect, beyond the mind itself; this story exists in the intuitive gaps between thought and intention. The fragments say what they need to say. They are cables, chains, and lariats leading carefully, providing support to get me where I need to go.

The Shape of Emptiness

His mother dies three weeks before the end of the quarter. A boy, a good student: he emails me to tell me the news, asks permission to be absent. *Of course*, I say, *take as much time as you need*. I tell him he can withdraw, take an incomplete, but he promises to be back in class next week. And he is.

I see him settled into his accustomed seat, his wire-rimmed glasses nestled securely on his nose, his khaki shirt buttoned, his feet encased in battered running shoes. I catch his eye, and we nod to one another, understanding. He needs to be here. The students flanking him know he needs to be here. A bright thread of tenderness coils around us.

We've been talking about white space. About the necessity of pause, of absence. The power of the gap. Of what is unsaid and unspeakable. I have nothing much more to tell them, these students who are winding their way toward their final projects, so I allow them to work with each other, to mull and brainstorm while I walk among them.

The boy sits attentively in his circle, making astute comments to the others. He leans forward on the small desk, crosses his forearms, tilts his head. I've told the students to be playful in this project, to use other media, to see it as a performance of all we've been learning about lyric forms. As a professor, I rarely feel in control, always feel like an imposter, that there's been a mistake. But with this particular class, there's a give and take in our discussions, an ease to our camaraderie; we've somehow become teachers to one another.

When the time comes for the presentations, the students rise to the task. One girl unfurls a quilt with sections of her essay printed on each square; she tells us she and her mom and her sisters stitched together this story of family over Thanksgiving. One girl has made her own soap and buried scraps of her essay inside the rough-hewn cakes. She brings in bowls of water and towels, asks us to wash our hands with her essay while she reads about shame, about wanting to be cleansed. She begins to cry, and I finish the recital for her.

The boy has brought in Play-Doh, small cans of it that he drops on each desk. He asks us to take the lump and squeeze it in our fists. That's all, just squeeze, then he gathers them up and puts these little sculptures on display at the front table. Each lump looks different, unique, modeling the individual shapes of our palms, the ridges from our inner knuckles.

The boy stands aside and begins to read, his voice soft at first then growing more forceful. He asks us: *What is the shape of emptiness?* Then he pauses, allows the question to remain unanswered. We gaze at our playdough impressions, see how we all have different ways to hang on. He made visible the air we never see. The shape of our holding, our hollow spaces pressed into clay. The form of the word, *please.*

Years from now, this boy will become a man. He'll marry and have two children, and I'll see the pictures on Facebook. He'll be my friend in the way many of us are friends these days: through screens and updates and thumbs-up. On the anniversary of his mother's death, he posts pictures, her face so like his own. I wonder if he remembers our classroom, the large windows that looked out toward the bay, the way light filtered in and made us all pause. I'll watch his hands as he carries one baby, then another, and see how full they have become.

But for now, when he finishes reading, he gathers our hands and gives them back to us one by one. We take them from him carefully, so we can carry our emptiness into the day. We compare them, showing off the shapes of our grasping. Curled like prayers. Like anger. Like love.

EPILOGUE

Collaboration in the Time of Covid-19

Brenda Miller and Julie Marie Wade

Author's note: Brenda Miller and Julie Marie Wade's piece "Notes from Isolation" was published online by *Green Mountains Review* on April 2, 2020, toward the start of quarantine measures in place for the Covid-19 pandemic. Here they describe their collaborative process on the essay.

BRENDA

I'm lying in bed after a fitful night's sleep, staring at my phone. It's become a bad habit, to pull my phone into bed with me on waking, searching out any form of communication: email, text, Instagram. Already I'm feeling lonely and alone, more so than usual, since self-isolation began in earnest a week ago. *Self* and *Isolation*: two words that now wed together uneasily, though for me they've always been convivial roommates.

And then I see, coming into view on my email queue, the name that always makes my heart glad: Julie Marie Wade. Julie was my graduate student decades ago; we'd kept in touch over the years, and then by serendipity, began collaborating on lyric essays. We've now written dozens of them, always starting with a simple word or phrase, writing quickly with a sense of play and discovery, making up rules and forms as we go along.

I open her message. It says, *Would you like to write an essay called "Notes from the Isolation Booth"?* Oh yes, I breathe, yes, yes, yes.

JULIE

In the beginning, I was thinking of the isolation booth as something positive: game-show contestants briefly sequestered but soon released to various reveries, among them the possibility of "winning big." This is how collaborating with Brenda has always seemed to me—a big win!—ever since we wrote our first essay together in the summer of 2015.

Brenda lives in northwestern Washington state, about twenty miles shy of the Canadian border, while I live in southeastern Florida, less than a hundred miles from the Keys. So we're already isolated from each other in the physical sense, but the words bring us close. The intimacy of the page somehow transcends the 3,300 miles between us—and at record speed. Collaboration is a kind of correspondence, after all, and these missives in a virtual bottle arrive just moments after one of us presses "send."

There's that sense of anticipation, too, which I imagine the game-show contestant feels as she waits inside a clear glass tube or just off-stage in a separate room, speculating about the imminent prizes. *What's being said?* she wonders. *What's soon to be revealed?* I'm gripped with a similar curiosity and delight each time I click the electronic paper clip next to Brenda's name. A little pause, to build suspense, and then the Word doc flickers open.

I suggested we change the name of our essay to "Notes from Isolation" only after I realized this time in our lives was not going to be brief, even by the most generous definition of the word. It wouldn't be much fun if the occupant of the isolation booth were told to eat and sleep inside, their release time perpetually postponed. And then, in an alarming twist, I read online that isolation booths are sometimes used in UK schools as punishments. They're a version of time-out where troublesome students are removed from class and placed in spare, silent rooms alone. This policy is also known as "occupy and ignore."

BRENDA

Julie begins by describing what she sees outside her window. I respond in kind with my own witnessing of the world as it passes by. This is how our collaborations often unfold: one of us begins with a small observation, the other picks it up and continues, and we pass our words back and forth, spurring each other on.

In this case, Julie has placed an asterisk after her short contemplation of the boats outside her ocean-view window. I study that asterisk—such a small thing but so powerful—and instinctively know I must make an effort to reach across it, this boundary, to connect. So I dip into Julie's section, picking up a few of her words as seeds for my own. I mirror the length and tone of her section as I explore the measure of our collective loneliness.

JULIE

A couple years ago, Brenda and I collaborated on an essay for the risk-themed issue of *Creative Nonfiction*. I remember that as we were writing together then, cataloging the many kinds of risks we encounter in our daily lives—but of course, never dreaming of the risks we face right now—I suddenly noticed the "risk" inside the word "asterisk." Heard it. Felt it. Wrote about it.

Here, perhaps, the asterisk—instead of a double space or another symbol to mark my section's end—was a semiconscious invocation of that sense of risk again. To collaborate is always to reach across a boundary between two separate lives and their unique, though often overlapping, experiences. Now in a time of profound isolation, reaching across this boundary feels more radical and necessary than ever before. Writing together is, paradoxically, the safest way and the riskiest way to connect with another person. Each entry exposes a little more vulnerability, plumbs a little deeper into its author's hopes and fears. The trust between Brenda and me, as writers and also now as friends, makes this literary intimacy possible.

BRENDA

We volley back and forth quickly, our sections expanding and deepening as we go along. A new routine materializes for me: I wake up—sometimes too early—and have my oatmeal and coffee, then, still wearing my bathrobe, settle into my couch with my second cup of coffee and read what Julie has sent me the day before. I do this before turning on the radio, before any other words can reach me.

I start a new section by picking up where Julie has left off. While the theme of isolation remains a murmur, our writing—as it always does—leads us further afield. My mother makes an appearance, as does my dead father. John Donne shows up alongside Virginia Woolf. I write about singing while Julie listens to R.E.M. on her daily run.

I write without stopping for a half hour. The house is quiet around me. My dog has gone back to sleep, her snores a soothing accompaniment. I write as if Julie is in the room with me, and she is. That is what collaboration means, even at a distance.

The last section I write begins with a phrase from a song I sing with my choir, *You are not alone. . . .* And I believe it now, more than ever, though my body is lonelier than it's ever been.

JULIE

It's been eighteen years since Brenda first introduced me to the lyric essay, in a "special topics" class on the genre. (*What if I hadn't signed up at all?*) I have learned so much from her: living in the same city and living on opposite sides of the country, writing together and writing apart. I feel Brenda's influence even and especially in my solo-authored work.

Right now my quarantine is a crowded one. A month ago, my partner began a permanent remote position as the technical support librarian for a college consortium. We never imagined I would soon be working exclusively from home as well, teaching lyric essay classes online in our bedroom while in our living room she teaches professors from other schools how to use their remote resources. Suddenly, we're tandem-Zooming! The apartment is noisier than ever before! The cats wander from workstation to workstation, making cameos on our visual calls, meowing at the strangers who smile back at them through the screen.

Collaboration is the quiet side of quarantine for me, a place I can retreat to when the world is too much with me, as it surely is now: construction workers on scaffolds just outside the high-rise windows; frantic emails from students who fear they are falling behind; aggressive hold Muzak played by the airlines; and of course, the news—*the news!* When I write with Brenda now, sometimes sitting on the cool tile floor in the bathroom with the door and blinds and windows closed, I can finally recollect in tranquility, begin to reckon with the larger isolation we are living now. Soon, there's a phone call, a cat scratching to come in. But briefly, I find my chosen isolation booth, the credo of which is "occupy and essay." Or, put another way—*be present and try.*

Sources

"Hand, Writing"

William Stafford, *The Way It Is: New and Selected Poems* (Graywolf Press, 1999).
Anne Carson, *Men in the Off Hours* (Vintage, 2001).

"The Case Against Metaphor: An Apologia"

Jane Hirshfield, *Nine Gates: Entering the Mind of Poetry* (Harper, 1997).
James Tate, "Introduction," *The Best American Poetry, 1997* (Scribner, 1997).

"A Braided Heart: Shaping the Lyric Essay"

Charles Simic, *Dime-Store Alchemy: The Art of Joseph Cornell* (New York Review Books Classics, 2006).
John D'Agata and Deborah Tall, *Seneca Review* 30th Anniversary Edition, "The Lyric Essay."

"A Case Against Courage in Creative Nonfiction"

Jill Christman, "The Sloth," *Brevity Magazine*, Issue 26, Winter 2008, ed. Dinty W. Moore. "The Sloth" is reprinted here by permission of the author.
Bernard Cooper, "Marketing Memory," from *The Business of Memory: The Art of Remembering in the Age of Forgetting*, ed. Charles Baxter (Graywolf Press, 1999).
Bernard Cooper, *Truth Serum* (Mariner Books, 1997).

Bill Moyers, Interview with Mark Doty, *Fooling with Words: A Celebration of Poets and Their Craft* (Harper, 2000).

Jill Sisson Quinn, "Subimago," *Bellingham Review*, Issue 54, Spring 2004, ed. Brenda Miller.

Sherry Simpson, "Fidelity," from *The Accidental Explorer* (Sasquatch Books, 2008).

Abigail Thomas, *Safekeeping* (Anchor, 2001).

"The Fine Art of Containment in Creative Nonfiction"

Virginia Woolf, "Street Haunting," *The Death of the Moth and Other Essays* (Harcourt, Brace & Company, 1942).

Ryan Van Meter, "First," *If You Knew Then What I Know Now* (Sarabande Books, 2011).

Brent Staples, "The Coroner's Photographs," *Parallel Time: Growing Up in Black and White* (Pantheon Books, 1994).

Bernard Cooper, "Burl's," *Truth Serum* (Mariner Books, 1997).

Karen Green, *Bough Down* (Siglio, 2013).

"The Shared Space Between Reader and Writer: A Case Study"

Brenda Miller, "We Regret to Inform You," in *An Earlier Life* (Judith Kitchen's Ovenbird Books, 2016).

"On Friendship, Assignments, Detail, and Trust"

Brenda Miller, "Swerve," in *An Earlier Life* (Judith Kitchen's Ovenbird Books, 2016).